Chakras,
Auras,
and the
New
Spirituality

Experience greater creativity
and spiritual abilities

Discover how to experience higher sources of energy and vibration through meditation with *Chakras, Auras, and the New Spirituality.* Once you have successfully become attuned to a higher spiritual vibration, you may find these energies expressed in your daily life as increased creativity and productivity, more altruistic philosophies, and greater mental and spiritual abilities.

This easy-to-follow guide presents a full-color aura section and 125 meditations designed to help you develop your spiritual abilities in a systematic way. It includes meditations on seeing auras, experiencing the "prism effect," visualizing health and prosperity, reaching mystical levels, developing your creativity and spiritual energy, and much more!

About the Authors

Genevieve Lewis Paulson and her son Stephen J. Paulson (Arkansas) are board members of Dimensions of Evolvement, Inc., a nonprofit growth center located in the Ozark Mountains. They both teach workshops and also work with individuals to help them further their personal and spiritual development.

To Write to the Authors

If you wish to contact the author or would like more information about this book, please write to the author in care of Llewellyn Worldwide and we will forward your request. Both the author and publisher appreciate hearing from you and learning of your enjoyment of this book and how it has helped you. Llewellyn Worldwide cannot guarantee that every letter written to the author can be answered, but all will be forwarded. Please write to:

Genevieve Lewis Paulson & Stephen J. Paulson
℅ Llewellyn Worldwide
P.O. Box 64383, 1-56718-513-4
St. Paul, MN 55164-0383, U.S.A.

Please enclose a self-addressed stamped envelope for reply,
or $1.00 to cover costs. If outside U.S.A., enclose
international postal reply coupon.

Many of Llewellyn's authors have websites with additional information and resources. For more information, please visit our website at
http://www.llewellyn.com

A Complete Guide to Opening the
Seven Senses

Chakras, Auras,

and the

New

Spirituality

Includes Full-Color Illustrations

Genevieve Lewis Paulson
& Stephen J. Paulson

2000
Llewellyn Publications
St. Paul, Minnesota 55164-0383, U.S.A.

First Edition
First Printing, 2000

Book design: Michael Maupin
Cover design: Lisa Novak
Illustrations: Mary Ann Zapalac

Chapter 4 aura photos on page 58
courtesy of Dixie Knight Photography, Little Rock, AR

Library of Congress Cataloging-in-Publication Data
Paulson, Genevieve Lewis, 1927 –
    Chakras, auras, and the new spirituality : a complete guide
    to opening the seven senses /
    Genevieve Lewis Paulson & Stephen J. Paulson.—1st ed.
        p.   cm.
Includes bibliographical references (p.   ) and index.
ISBN 1-56718-513-4
    1. Chakras. 2. Aura. 3. Spirituality. I. Paulson, Stephen J.
    II. Title.
BL1215.C45 P38 2000
131—dc21   00-045288

Llewellyn Publications
A Division of Llewellyn Worldwide, Ltd.
P. O. Box 64383, 1-56718-513-4
St. Paul, MN 55164-0383, U.S.A.
www.llewellyn.com

Printed in the United States of America

Other books by Genevieve Lewis Paulson:

Energy-Focused Meditation

Kundalini and the Chakras

with Stephen J. Paulson:

Reincarnation: Remembering Past Lives

Dedication

This book is dedicated to our children and grandchildren:

Genevieve's Children

Stephen

Kari

Nina

Brad

Roger

Grandchildren

Wendy

Matthew

Daniel

Noel

Brian

Ariel

Jessica

Elijah

Hannah

Nathan

Stephen's Children

Wendy

Noel

Brian

Elijah

Hannah

Grandchildren

Amber Lynn

Alexi Kay

Kristen Maxx

Tyler Lawrence

Genevieve also wishes to dedicate
this book to her Godchild—Cooper Moon

Our thanks to Roger S. Paulson
for sharing his insights on eyes three through seven.
Stephen thanks his wife, RaeJean, for her patience and love.
Thanks also to Ralph Thiel,
who so patiently put this manuscript on computer.

We appreciate, also, our workshop participants who through the years have explored these areas with us. Special appreciation goes to the Indy-Ucky Kundalini Group, formed in 1980 and still growing strong.

Contents

Chapter 9: The Spherical System   141

Chapter 10: Developing the Spheres   163

Chapter 11: Using the Energies   193

Meditations

Chapter 1

Chapter 2

Chapter 3

Chapter 4

Chapter 5

Chapter 6

Chapter 10 (continued)

Introduction

THERE IS A New Spirituality penetrating our common consciousness, opening us to a greater way of being—something similar to a major upgrade for your computer. There will be new things you can do and comprehend. There will be more information, creativity, and inventiveness available to people. This energy will also cause realities, previously separate from our daily consciousness, to be more of an integral part of our being. For example, the concept of reincarnation, time, space, and parallel dimensions are already coming into the mainstream of consciousness. The wave of energies that caused the "New Age" appeared during the 1960s and 1970s. It was a wonderful opening. However, the energies tended to be somewhat flaky and not very practical. It was harder to sort out and use those energies. The wave of energy, which began in 1999 and is continuing and increasing into the new millennium, is bringing this New Spirituality, which has a greater sense of groundedness and usefulness. It is a much more practical energy and will help people make greater "upgrades" in their lives. We will be more open to new, far-reaching philosophies and concepts.

Sevens and Twelves

It is interesting to note how the numerals 7 and 12 permeate our lives. For instance, there are seven days in a week, twelve months in a year, seven notes in a scale, and twelve if you include the sharps (or flats). In earlier astrology, seven planets were known including the Sun, Moon, Mercury, Venus, Mars, Jupiter, and Saturn. Since then Uranus, Neptune, Pluto, and Chiron have been discovered and are included. If we add Earth to this number (and we should since we are sitting on it), then the number becomes twelve. Kundalini (evolutionary energy) begins with seven main chakras. We've included a number of sevens and some twelves. Some readers, we're sure, will be able to think of many more instances of the uses of sevens and twelves in our lives.

Faith Javane and Dusty Bunker write that "persons" with the number 7 will search for your own individual belief system. They also report that Pythagoras considered 7 to be the most sacred of all numbers, and that it is the principle number in the Bible, used well over 350 times. The number 12 is also used many times in the Bible, representing completeness. For the number 12, on the individual level they indicate that you are an unusual person who has accumulated inner strength through your unique experience. They also indicate that the "number 12 belongs to the developed soul."* We certainly agree with their assessments of the numbers and since 7 and 12 have such high, positive energies for growth and development, it stands to reason that by focusing on these

* *Numerology and the Divine Triangle* by Faith Javane and Dusty Bunker; Whitford Press: West Chester, PA, 1979.

numbers their vibration will help to bring in their energies. We have also found great organizational energies available for higher work under the 12 vibration. In our work we have noticed that the two numbers in some strange way have a rhythm with one another, and that if you work to develop your seven energies, you will open more to the energies of 12. Of the numeral 12: "It is related to 7, another number of completeness, because both are made of 3 and 4 . . . and both are regarded by the numerologically minded as linked with the essential underlying structure of the universe."* Both 7 and 12 have energies of completion. Although 12 is not as popular a number in spiritual growth and development at this time, we believe that as we progress further into the Aquarian Age it will be focused on as much as 7 is now and, perhaps, more. One shouldn't take the sevens and twelves so seriously, however, that systems with other numbers aren't explored and experienced. No matter what the numbers, they all represent growth. Sometimes it is more in the human levels and sometimes more in the spiritual levels; we do need both.

Focus of Growth

Some people feel that their focus should be entirely on spiritual growth, and this may be true of certain persons for this life. However, generally speaking, we are here to develop our bodies as well. We are in these bodies for a reason and not just to absolve karma. If our only reason for existence were to absolve karma, there wouldn't be much point in starting the process! There has to be a greater reason for being here; for evolution of the species and the individual, to bring us into fullness of being in the spiritual world. School systems focus on mental, and sometimes physical, education. Due to violence and individual problems, they are opening up to the emotional, too. The importance of the spirit or spiritual will have to be included as well. That is difficult, however, as the religious institutions feel that is their department. Religion does need

* *Man, Myth and Magic*, Richard Cavendish, editor; Marshall Cavendish Corporation: New York, NY, 1970.

to be separate from schools, however, one's spirit needs to be included, especially through creativity and expression. Religious institutions need also to open more to the spiritual and not just the form of religion and its rules. People today are in desperate need to go beyond, into the greater spiritual/mystical areas. Sometimes they have to go it alone or carve out their own niche someplace in the world. This happens to all great mystics, scientists, inventors, philosophers, or others who have much to offer the world. They must have the courage and dedication to go beyond what is currently available. And there aren't too many people out there to hold their hands, either!

In the area sometimes called "New Age," many groups are forming and leaders coming forth to help in this push beyond our current evolutionary status. Their effect has been strong and supportive for many in their changes. Whether you are alone, or participate in groups, we hope this book brings more awareness of the spiritual rhythm of these two numbers and provides information and experiences related to some of the different ways they affect us in our evolutionary journey.

How to Use the Meditations in this Book

Many of the chapters contain meditations so you can experience the information in the book and not just read it. The information becomes much more important when it is viewed through one's own experiences. Generally, preparation for the meditations is not provided because some people have their own methods for this. Actually too much preparation, if it balances and clears a person too much, can slow down the information coming through. Sometimes minimal relaxation is all that is necessary. Also, some people like to have journals or notebooks in which to put information received. If you do not have a preparation for meditation exercise, the following may be helpful:

Meditation Preparation

1. Read through the exercise first so that you are aware of its contents, or have someone lead you through it. Some people like to tape the instructions and follow that.

2. Lie down or sit comfortably with the back and head straight. Comfort is necessary, otherwise, you may be distracted by aches and pains.

3. Take some deep, but peaceful breaths and let loose of your body so that energy may flow easily.

4. Begin focusing on the mediation.

Everyone's energy is expanding in one area or another, but, especially, in the spiritual area. We need to have opportunities to use this extra energy. This book gives suggestions and areas in which to make the new energies and new growth usable.

Chapter 1

The
Seven
Bodies

We humans, in our evolvement back to our divine source, have been given seven bodies through which to develop and expand awareness. The seven bodies are interpenetrating and composed of energy vibrating at different rates (see Figure 1.1, page 3). The energy attracts etheric matter of like nature to it, to form the bodies. The densest of these bodies, and the only one readily seen, is the physical body. The other bodies, vibrating at correspondingly higher rates, are the emotional, mental, intuitional, will/spirit, soul, and divine bodies. People are, however, not just these seven bodies. They are pure consciousness, which can reside in any body or combination of bodies. In this particular age there are very few persons whose consciousness is so developed or their bodies so vivified, or attuned that they can function in all bodies at

1

one time. This is the ultimate goal, that can be reached in the earthly development. As a person can function in all bodies at once, that is, all bodies in harmony with an individual's consciousness, then that person will be living as perfect a life as is possible on this earth.

In primitive people, the physical and emotional bodies were being developed and trained to respond to man's consciousness. There were the first stirrings in the mental body and as humanity progressed through the ages, the higher bodies were awakened and their development begun. It is much the same as a newborn baby learning to develop her muscles, her awareness, and then to function in the world. In this age, people are beginning to learn to function in these higher bodies.

Bodies and Their Functions

Our bodies are composed of matter, vibrating at particular speeds, each one relating to a different level and having different functions. Thus each level, or body, is a vehicle for expression of various states of consciousness.

Physical Body

All bodies have higher and lower levels. In the case of the physical body, we can readily see the lower form because of its density. The physical body is a living machine through which our higher bodies express themselves and our individual consciousness, besides expressing itself, can with intent, transmute energies. Our bodies are designed to be *transformers* of energy.

Its higher form is the etheric body which hasn't manifested into denser form, but is made up of an energy web which can absorb light and higher energies to energize and heal the lower physical body. The etheric is just slightly larger than the physical, however, maintaining the same basic shape. It is, therefore, sometimes called the etheric double. A strong, well-developed etheric helps a person be and feel more dynamic. We will discuss the etheric body in more detail in chapter 4.

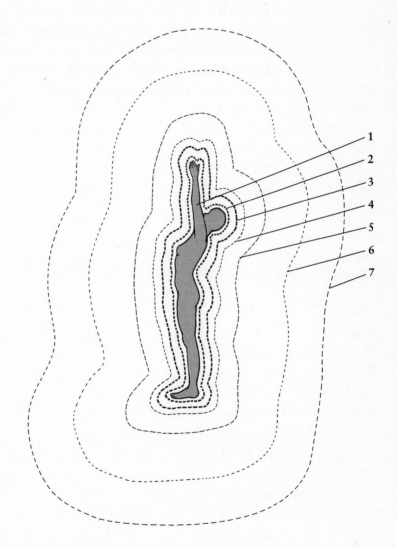

Figure 1.1 The Seven Bodies

1—Physical Body; 2—Emotional Body; 3—Mental Body; 4—Intuitional/Compassionate Body; 5—Will/Spirit Body; 6—Soul Body; 7—Divine Body

As we block off our physical body, we also block the expressions of our higher selves. We can feel, or think, a good deal, but if the expression or action is denied, we become frustrated and further problems can occur. Many problems, which manifest in the physical body as aches, pains, or illnesses, are simply what happens to the physical body when blocks prevent the expressions from the higher bodies. Such examples include ulcers from tensions, because expressions such as anger or frustration are not released; constipation, because we emotionally or mentally hold onto something; liver problems, caused when we do not act on matters of the spiritual side of life. Cancers are sometimes caused by cells in revolt. They can no longer function as they were meant to, but begin to grow wildly and out of control, in essence setting up their own community. There are numerous other examples of the body under stress.

The physical body is composed of cells which have their own individuality and should be under our conscious control; not a dominating control, but a loving control. If one considers our bodies as universes unto themselves, then we are lords of our universes. We then can realize at a greater depth the responsibility we have for the development of our physical body as well as our higher bodies. The etheric or higher form of the physical is very closely connected with our nervous system. Where we refer to the physical body in this book, unless otherwise indicated, we are including the etheric level, too. They are so closely related that what affects one, affects the other.

Emotional Body

The emotional body is where our feelings emanate. This is where we feel anger and frustrations if our needs are not met, where we learn to give and express love and caring, thus fulfilling our needs to be in relationship with others. It is a very demanding body, which will seek to have its needs met through various ways, if not directly. When it feels depleted or unable to express, it may seek balance in smoking, overeating certain foods, irrational behavior, or other ways of gratifying itself. On this level emotions can conflict with one another, be heavily affected by the subconscious, and reactions to information and desires from higher bodies. This body expresses itself as emotion, including pleasure, excitement, and emotional pain. It is much better if we can have direct contact with our emotions, to know what is going on, and be able to deal with the needs of the emotional body in more fulfilling ways.

This body is very closely related to the divine body and is where we begin to feel divine love and caring.

Mental Body

The mental body contains matter vibrating at a similar rate to the creative force in our cosmos. It is where we begin to think, to reason, to know. It is a body through which we gather knowledge and, through reason and logic, apply this knowledge. It is also the body where we set up rigid attitudes or structures in our system. It is the area where prejudices are formed. The more rigid the matter in our mental body becomes, the more difficult it is to flow with life, learn new ways of living, and acquire new ideas.

The ego resides on the mental level and has charge of developing the personality (physical, emotional, and mental). If it doesn't allow energy and insights to flow down from the higher bodies for guidance, it will tend to become more and more rigid and defensive in order to keep a tight control and eventually tries to control the entire system. The ideal way for our ego to develop is in opening up to our higher bodies, letting the higher self and soul flow through, letting our spirit flow through. The ego then becomes a channel for our spiritual bodies (intuitional/compassionate, will/spirit, and divine) to flow through into the personality bodies. The mental body sometimes wants to shut off expressions of emotional and physical bodies. The higher level of the mental body brings genius level abilities and connection to the universal mind.

Intuitional/Compassionate Body

This is the first of the four bodies we consider as our spiritual self, rather than personality self. It is the vehicle for contact with the universal mind, which gives us insight and understanding, and is the source of abstract thinking, rather than the concrete, logical thinking of the mental body.

The intuitional body is also the body of understanding and compassion. It is sometimes called the "buddhic" body, after the compassionate Buddha. One can feel compassion from this level because of the understanding available to us through this level, the home of intuition and compassion. The higher level of this body brings us a great sense of connection with other humans.

Will/Spirit Body

Little understood, the will/spirit body is where we express our spirit and our will. It is the body through which we sow much karma as there is a strong force behind anything which comes from this area. It gives us charisma. It is also the body that can force its will upon others. It is the source of energy keeping us going when all else is depleted.

The will/spirit body is the home of sex. It is where our negative and positive polarities are separated and seek union with opposite polarities. This need for union with opposite polarity may be expressed through sex, but more commonly is expressed through the vibrational interchange between two persons' sets of their seven bodies.

The higher level of this body can bring great power and strong charisma.

Soul Body

This body expresses the unity of the polarities in this body. This unity allows the soul to express itself in this body. When this body is fully developed, it then becomes a receptacle of soul energy, which energizes and uplifts the system to a higher level (from solar to galactic, or galactic to universal, etc.). We receive the essence of our "I Am-ness" at this level. At this level, neither adversities nor success touches us—we just *are*.

When the higher level is developed we will flow through life with detachment and freedom. At the same time there will be great connections with others and the universe through essence.

Divine Body

To divine is to know the will of God for oneself. This body is our most direct point of contact with our Divine Source. As we develop here, we begin to experience the oneness with God and with the entire universe. Living with all bodies being permeated with a flow from the divine body is to be living in constant oneness with God. This is a divine consciousness. Persons with the higher levels developed will have God-like attributes and abilities.

Living With, In, and Through Our Bodies

All bodies interpenetrate the physical body, except during such periods as out-of-the-body travel. The emotional body, sometimes called the astral body, is the one most commonly used for out-of-body travel. As a person develops in his or her consciousness, higher bodies may be used for this type of travel.

Each of our bodies develops its own awareness and its own "mind," with its own fears, attitudes, and can—if given enough energy—try to control the entire system. This can hinder your growth. The bodies need to learn to share energies, share decisions, and to live with each other. Energy concentrated in one or two bodies indicates control of the system by those particular bodies. If persons are primarily into their emotional body, then they will react with themselves and their environment almost totally from the emotional level. If they function from the mental level, then the approach will be through the mind. This type of functioning is limiting and not very fulfilling or satisfying. A person may become so frustrated from the one-sided living that he or she may go out of character and begin relating from another body. Awareness and contact with all bodies is necessary for a full life. Without it there may be ambivalence and confusion.

As we cleanse our systems, our spirit is better able to flow. We find we will act in ways appropriate to our life situations. We will be aware of the freedom of life flowing in and from us.

Cleansing and Developing Meditations

There are a number of energies affecting us in various ways. Each of these energies have their own particular form or pattern. They can, however, manifest as color, sound, smell, feeling, information, or as sustenance for our bodies. These energies and their manifestations or emanations affect our bodies. In this first exercise we are using color and sound emanations to cause the particular bodies to vibrate. This, in turn, helps us get in touch with each body, to help in awareness cleansing and development.

Meditation 1: Basic Bodies

Using the following chart, fill each body, in turn, with the color and sound indicated. Hold the color and sound for one or two minutes in the beginning. As you develop you will find it more profitable to hold the colors and sounds for longer periods of time. With this exercise, your emotional and mental blocks may release faster than your system can easily handle. Irritability, or flu-like symptoms, may result from excessive releasing. If this happens, stop for a while.

Different colors and sounds are used for the bodies when they become more refined and respond to the energies from higher sources. Following are colors and sounds used when the person is responding primarily to energies from our solar system. (In the following chapters information will be given for bodies responding to galactic, universal, and cosmic energies.)

Body	Color	Sound
Physical	Camel Tan with White Clouds	*ah*
Emotional	Apple Green with White Clouds	*en*
Mental	Lavender with White Clouds	*oh*
Intuitional	Light Blue with Silver Streaks	*eh*
Will/Spirit	Mauve with Silver Streaks	*oh'la*
Soul	Light Gold with Silver Streaks	*ah'men*
Divine	White Fire with Silver Streaks	*ohm*

Chart 1.1 Color and Sound Chart for Solar Bodies

Meditation 2: House of the Seven Bodies

This exercise deals in a symbolic way whether or not we live in our bodies and our attitudes towards them. Have some paper and a pencil handy to write down your impressions.

Either lie down or sit comfortably, with eyes closed. Breathe peacefully and deeply and fill yourself with a camel tan with clouds of white for a few minutes, keeping your awareness on your breathing and the color. Then, letting your awareness leave your breathing and the color, visualize a house with seven rooms, one for each body.

First, enter the room for the physical body. What does it look like? What colors are used? How is it decorated? Are you comfortable there? Does it look lived in? Do not make any changes at this time, but write down your impressions and then continue through the rooms, always writing down your impressions. Use the same format before going into each room, using the colors and sounds from the solar body chart.

After finishing the exercise, look at your notes. Which body seems to be lived in most? Which least? Where do you sense problems?

Repeat the exercise, this time changing the rooms in any way you would like. (You may feel physically tired and wish to leave this part until you have rested.)

You may wish to keep a record of this and repeat the exercise at a future date and see if you have made some changes of a more permanent nature.

Meditation 3: You Are Not Your Bodies

Lie down, or sit comfortably. Keep your attention on your breathing for a few minutes; let it be peaceful and deep. Then let your attention leave your breathing and be aware that you are pure consciousness. You are not your bodies. You are pure consciousness which has been given seven types of matter so that you may energize them and learn to function through them. Get the feeling of your pure consciousness moving in and out of the bodies. Get the feeling of what it will be like when your consciousness is so developed that it can function and be in all bodies at once. Practice being in all your bodies at once. Let your breathing be expanded, enjoy the feeling. Try to remember this feeling so that you may carry it with you in your daily life. End the meditation by stretching.

Meditation 4: Color Meditation for Cleansing and Developing Awareness of Bodies

Lie down or sit comfortably, keeping your attention on deep, peaceful breathing for a few minutes. Then let your awareness *be centered on your physical body,* let yourself be filled with the camel tan with clouds of white coming through, say "ah" to yourself several times. Be aware of your physical body for a few minutes. Continue with each of the bodies, using the color and sound chart.

Meditation 5: Color Meditation for Unifying Bodies

Do the previous meditation, "Color Meditation for Cleansing and Developing Awareness of Bodies." When you have completed the meditation, go from the divine level into the monadic level and bring the color for the divine body into the soul level. Then be in the will/spirit level and fill it with the color for the divine body. Continue this until you have been in touch with each body and filled it with the white fire with the bluish cast and silver streaming through. *Let yourself feel totally aware and unified.* Stretch, but try to retain the unified feeling within you.

Meditation 6: Love, Peace, and Brotherhood

Lie down or sit comfortably, breathing peacefully and deeply. Fill yourself with the color and sound for each body in turn. When you are in touch with each particular body, spend a few minutes feeling love, peace, and brotherhood and then go on to the next body. We need to be able to feel love, peace, and brotherhood in our entire system.

Meditation 7: Care of Your Bodies— The Labor/Management Exercise

Lie down or sit comfortably breathing peacefully and deeply. Fill yourself with the color and sound for each body in turn, beginning with the physical. Be the person in charge and talk with each body to see what needs it may have and what you can do to help it. Follow through where you think it is advisable. If you don't think a request is advisable, explain to the body and come to an agreement. Ask each body the following questions: Do you get enough exercise? Do you have a proper diet? Do you get proper rest? What needs to do you have?

Be at peace with your bodies.

The Seven Planes

Chart 1.2, on the following page, shows the seven planes of our evolvement as humans, from primitive consciousness to cosmic consciousness. In each of the seven planes you will note there are seven subplanes with similar characteristics. Also, in each of these subplanes there are seven more subplanes (not shown) which have similar characteristics to the large subplanes and planes. Thus we work with our physical, emotional, mental, intuitional/compassionate, will/spirit, soul, and divine faculties over and over again through the evolutionary process.

At the present time, we have just entered the Age of Aquarius. Average people will now be able to use the energies from the galaxy for his evolvement. We may now call ourselves "galactic humans." In the Age of Pisces, through which we have just passed, the highest source of energy average people had available to them was solar energy, thus we call them: "solar humans." Average people will now develop on plane five during this Aquarian Age, which will last approximately 2,500 years. Then humanity will progress to plane six. There are, of course those more highly evolved beings who are an age or more ahead of the average person. We are given the choice of speeding our growth through our

No.	Age	Main Energy Source	Primary Level of Development	Subplane Polarity	
				Positive	Negative
7	Sagittarius	Cosmos	Divine		Divine (-) Soul (+) Will/Spirit (+) Intuitional (-) Mental (+) Emotional (-) Physical (+)
6	Capricorn	Universe	Soul	Divine (-) Soul (+) Will/Spirit (+) Intuitional (-) Mental (+) Emotional (-) Physical (+)	
5	Aquarius	Galaxy	Will/Spirit	Divine (-) Soul (+) Will/Spirit (+) Intuitional (-) Mental (+) Emotional (-) Physical (+)	
4	Pisces	Solar	Intuitional		Divine (-) Soul (+) Will/Spirit (+) Intuitional (-) Mental (+) Emotional (-) Physical (+)
3	Aries	Planetary	Mental	Divine (-) Soul (+) Will/Spirit (+) Intuitional (-) Mental (+) Emotional (-) Physical (+)	
2	Taurus	Moon	Emotional		Divine (-) Soul (+) Will/Spirit (+) Intuitional (-) Mental (+) Emotional (-) Physical (+)
1	Gemini	Earth	Physical	Divine (-) Soul (+) Will/Spirit (+) Intuitional (-) Mental (+) Emotional (-) Physical (+)	

Chart 1.2 Planes of Evolution of Human Consciousness

efforts or delaying our growth through disinterest, excessive interest in the personality, or through engendering excessive karma (karma means actions are followed by reactions, or "you reap what you sow"). The choice is always ours. Those who have gone beyond the galactic energy in their growth will be using the energy of the universe, or even the cosmos, thus reaching cosmic consciousness. Anyone working on his or her spiritual growth will be tapping into these higher energies at times.

Turning again to the chart of the seven planes of evolution, please note the spiraling effect of our growth. Each level has a positive or negative polarity. This causes us to flow back and forth through a positive or negative influence. You will note we are leaving a negative age which meant much introspection and looking within, and are reaching into the positive influence of the galactic age. People will look more outward. More people will tend to find answers in relationships with others and to the world, rather than for just themselves. This can be called an *action* age. People of the twentieth century have been feeling the influence of this galactic age as they began exploring outer space, and through the process of spiritual expansion.

On the chart you will note there are two positive planes together. This serves a very useful purpose in helping give us the push from one age to the next. Where positive and negative are together they pull together. The two positives together, for instance, on subplanes five and six of plane four, help give the added push we need to be in the galactic age. Those who have reached soul levels in their meditations may remember crossing through a barrier to reach the other level. For some it results in a momentary lapse of consciousness, some experience an erasing of the consciousness, much like the erasing of a blackboard, and for others it is like breaking through a heavenly barrier.

One might also be aware that after plane seven is reached there are more planes for evolvement in the heavens beyond the heavens.

Also, previous to our development on plane one, there were similar though less evolved planes through which to develop.

You will note that only seven of the astrological signs are used in this chart. The other five astrological signs are present in previous stages of evolvement not covered in this book.

Moving from Solar to Galactic Influences

In the Aquarian Age the stronger, more penetrating energies of the galaxy and newly discovered distant planets of our solar system will increasingly affect us. These may be referred to as "new rays" of energy. They are new in the sense they are not currently considered in most astrology charts. They are also new in that many people have been unaffected by them prior to the Aquarian Age. In the orbit of the sun through the galaxy we are now in relation to new energies, and through astrological changes, we then will be even more open to the influence of these galactic energies. These rays of energy are "old" in the sense they have existed since the beginning of our galaxy and they are "old" in the sense that more highly evolved persons have been able to use these energies prior to the Aquarian Age, which may also be called the "Galactic Age."

Since the pervading energies of the Galactic Age will be of the positive or active form rather than the negative/passive, we will find that it is much more difficult to block emotional feelings or to adhere to our rigid mental structures through which we previously operated. We will seek new lifestyles and new freedom of expression. It will be a time of great creativity in all areas. It will be a more general rule for people to have some creative expression and to actively use it than in the previous ages. The creative expression will not just manifest through the arts but in all of our daily lives. It will be increasingly difficult for anyone to be in an occupation which does not allow freedom of creative expression.

This creative expression will also reach into relationships and lifestyles. It will mean cleaning out of the old blocks carried in one's personality, some of which were formed in this life and some of which were formed in previous lives. This is necessary so that our systems can handle the new galactic energies. If we do not cleanse ourselves, the galactic energies, which are stronger and more penetrating, will *force* a cleansing. If we still resist this, then we may find ourselves physically ill, as the problems manifest through the body as illnesses, or we may experience emotional or mental depressions or breakdowns and it may be difficult to function in the everyday world due to the stress.

With the galactic energies, we will find it is much easier to voice our opinions, to act upon our desires or needs. In time past, we were freer to think about things and daydream about them more. In this age, *action* is the key word. It is also a time when more karma can be sown due to the stronger galactic energies that will be used in our actions. It becomes more imperative that we are aware of what we are feeling, what our subconscious and conscious motives are, simply because of the force behind all that we think or feel. We will not be able to hide our inner selves as well as we could during the Piscean, or Solar, Age. This has its good side, also. We will become more understanding of others as we become more understanding of ourselves. People will feel much freer to live in the way they choose. "Society" will not be as strong an influence.

During this time of galactic energy, we will be working to refine our intuitional and compassionate abilities so that we can use the will/spirit forces easier. One needs to be able to use the past energy flows before being able to develop the attributes for that particular age. The intuitional, compassionate qualities will be much needed as we expand in the galactic energy field.

For solar humans, certain colors and sounds were given to help our bodies vibrate at that particular level. As galactic humans, another set of colors is given to help refine the matter in the bodies and to cleanse out all blocks so that the bodies can vibrate to the energy from the galaxy (see Chart 1.3, next page). Work with the solar colors is necessary first to help in the cleansing so it is

Body	Color	Sound
Physical	Light Gold Fire with Silver Streaks	*ah'men*
Emotional	White Fire with Silver Streaks	*ohm*
Mental	Orange with Gold and Silver Streaks	*rahmah*
Intuitional	Peach with Gold Flecks	*mahran*
Will/Spirit	Bright Blue with Gold Flecks	*elah*
Soul	Emerald Green with Gold Flecks	*dahlan*
Divine	Lavender with Reddish-Violet cast	*aum*

Chart 1.3 Color and Sound Chart for Galactic Bodies

not as toxic to the system when old feelings, thoughts, and attitudes are released. Work with the colors and sounds for galactic humans should be used for the refining and any cleansing remaining. It is difficult to cleanse all from an age just past; much is taken with us into the new age. It is easier on us if we can clean all that's possible. This allows us to open to the new higher energies in a way that will help us to live a much deeper, richer life. When we have cleansed and refined our solar bodies, they will begin to vibrate at the higher rate of the galactic energies. We may then say our bodies are "an octave higher." The following chart shows colors and sounds that aid us in vibrating and relating to the galactic energies in our various bodies.

You will note the colors and sounds for the physical and emotional bodies of the galactic system are the same as the monadic and divine of the solar bodies respectively. The matter of the solar monadic body becomes the basis for the physical galactic body. The matter of the solar divine body becomes the basis for the emotional galactic body. Thus we never totally enter into a new, unexplored set of bodies. There is always a foundation on which to build. Note: In galactic meditations it may be easier to keep your eyes open, due to energy force.

Meditation 8: Cleansing and Developing Awareness in Bodies at a Galactic Level

Lie down or sit comfortably, breathing peacefully and deeply. Be aware of your pure consciousness, then fill yourself with the sound and color of each body in turn, filling it with your consciousness and awareness. (Sometimes you may see past-life situations during this exercise.)

Meditation 9: For Various Information

Follow the above exercise, and when you have the awareness in your body you may ask the body various questions, such as: What is my relationship with this person (name someone)? What do I want to give and receive in this relationship? What is my relationship to God? What do I want to do with my life?

This exercise may be used in a number of ways beyond those mentioned above. It is a good way to get in touch with your indecision in matters. You may find each of the seven bodies have different answers, or you may find that all are in accord except one. It is a very interesting, practical way of finding out how we do or do not function and what some of the reasons may be for our behaviors.

Meditation 10: Destiny Trip

Follow the basic color and sounds (see Chart 1.3 on page 17) and ask each body what it feels its destiny is in this life. Then ask your pure consciousness what it thinks its destiny is. Then talk with each body, in turn, beginning with the physical and try to reach an accord. If all are working toward the same destiny, you may get there.

Meditation 11: Let Spirit Flow

Since the Galactic Age is one of will/spirit energies, it is a time to let one's spirit flow. Follow the basic colors listed in the galactic chart and let your spirit flow through each body. Visualize yourself functioning in each body and let spirit flow through the functioning.

Ages of the Future

Many people who have dedicated themselves to their spiritual growth are functioning in varying degrees on the universal and cosmic planes. Some are reaching the higher levels in their meditations, but live their lives vibrating to the solar energies. If there is too great a disparity between the meditational levels and the level of daily life, disorientation can be the result.

It is recommended that you use the higher colors with caution so as not to disrupt the system unduly.

Universal Bodies

Chart 1.4 contains the colors for the bodies vibrating at the universal level. Sounds are not given for the universal and cosmic bodies. Sounding the vowels may be helpful for any of the universal bodies and should be used at the discretion of the meditator.

Body	Color
Physical	Emerald Green with Gold Flecks
Emotional	Lavender with Reddish-Violet cast and Gold Flecks
Mental	Aqua-Green and Yellow Patches
Intuitional	Fuschia and Orange Patches
Will/Spirit	Ruby Red with Diamond Flecks
Soul	Indigo with Diamond Flecks
Divine	Brilliant White

Chart 1.4 Colors for the Bodies of Universal People

Meditation 12: Universal Color

Use the color chart for the universal bodies. Do not use the colors for more than a few minutes each at the beginning. If you notice anger or irritation arising when you use the ruby red with diamonds, fill yourself with love. After anger and irritation are cleansed from the system, ruby red will fill a person with pure energy, to be used in a variety of ways.

At the universal level the bodies begin to merge with one another, sometimes causing combinations of the colors.

Body	Color
Physical	Very Light Rose
Emotional	Very Light Salmon
Mental	Very Light Yellow
Intuitional	Very Light Green
Will/Spirit	Very Light Blue
Soul	Very Light Lavender
Divine	Radiant Light

Chart 1.5 Colors for the Cosmic Person

Cosmic Level

On the cosmic level, it is difficult to separate the specific bodies due to the oneness of the system at this level. The color for the cosmic system is a radiant white with bright pastel colors undulating over the radiance. (See Chart 1.5, above.)

Sounds such as waterfalls, bells, music, or wind are sometimes heard when meditating at this level.

Meditation 13: Cosmic Energies

1. Lie down, or sit comfortably. Breathe deeply. Be aware only of a radiant white, completely filling

you. Be aware of any coloring over the white or of any sounds, but do not concentrate on them. Keep your concentration on the radiance no more than three minutes at a time, in the beginning. If you find your nerves are bothered, discontinue the exercise until more cleansing can be done.

2. Be aware of any sounds.

3. Be in an open meditation to let thoughts and feelings emerge.

Completion of Evolutionary Path

When evolutionary periods are completed, those persons who have not completed the necessary development will repeat the evolutionary path. They will do this until they have developed sufficiently to enter a higher evolutionary plan.

As mentioned previously, a person who is willing to devote his or her life to the spiritual path may speed up the evolutionary process. For instance, one need not wait for the Age of Capricorn to be in the Universal Age, nor do we need to wait for the Age of Sagittarius to be in the Divine Age. Sometimes excessive amounts of karma can hold us back from making much progress, but if we are dedicated to growing and developing, we can move along at a much faster pace. As we learn to control and develop each level of our systems, our pure consciousness, our self becomes more expanded and developed until we are into our full God-consciousness and become active participating units of creation. We will be one with our Divine Source.

Chapter 2

Beyond the Seven Bodies

BODIES EIGHT THROUGH twelve and beyond are higher levels of the basic seven vibrations that we call bodies. This is an example of seven pushing us into twelve. In this chapter we will explore the higher octaves, or levels, of these basic bodies.

Exploring the Bodies

Through the quantum leaps of the 1980s and 1990s, many people find they are functioning in these higher vibrations. There is still a need to be sure the basic seven are open and functioning, however, since failure to do so will cause problems at the higher levels. Usually the higher levels won't open unless the basic ones are fully developed. However, with the almost magical lifting of

Basic Function			Beyond Levels			
Physical	1	6	11	16	21	26
Emotional	2	7	12	17	22	27
Mental	3	8	13	18	23	28
Intuitional	4	9	14	19	24	29
Will/Spirit	5	10	15	20	25	30
Soul	6	11	16	21	26	31
Divine	7	12	17	22	27	32

Chart 2.1 Levels Beyond the Seven Bodies

human consciousness levels, happening in the end of the twentieth century and the beginning of the twenty-first century, the higher ones are being activated. Also, some persons who in previous lives would have achieved very high spiritual levels will find that these levels are being reactivated. This can bring confusion as to how to work with person's consciousness, since it will vary from day to day. Chart 2.1 above shows how the process of raising consciousness to higher levels works. When a person achieves the higher vibration, the qualities of his bodies change somewhat. Actually, we only have five basic levels and the changes begin with levels six and seven. They are higher levels of one and two. The reason for working with seven rather than five is that it then begins to pull us up to the next spiral. The total then becomes twelve. Following is a list of the bodies and their higher level purposes:

6—Soul

The sixth, or soul, level relates to the soul manifesting in the body so that growth can be achieved through it for the benefit of the soul. When the physical body is raised in vibration from one to six, the body will be lighter, look more youthful, and will be more disease-free.

7—Divine

The seventh level is a higher level of the second or emotional/feeling body and represents how we connect with the Divine heart of God through emotions/feelings. The emotional level when lifted to the seventh-level vibration causes emotions and feelings to become more lighter, more joyful, and also, more meaningful.

8—God's Miracle Level

The eighth level is a higher level of the third, which relates to the mental. It is the gateway to the mind of God. It is able through mental strength to open to miracles. It can bring great strength to any level and helps with healing through changing attitudes and other mental processes. When the mental body is lifted to the vibration of the eighth level, one can see the bigger picture of life better, be more creative, and lose prejudices because of greater comprehension.

9—As Above, So Below

This is the level which helps us intuit and understand spiritual concepts and how they are used on the human level. It is a higher level of the intuitional/compassionate level. When the intuitional/compassionate level is raised in vibrations to the ninth level, understanding is greatly expanded and compassion becomes stronger, but does not interfere with the other person's path and growth.

10—Power of All-Consuming Love

This is the higher level of the fifth level. It is filled with the power of all-consuming love. When the will/spirit (fifth level) is raised in vibration to the tenth level, a person's life will change—the focus of love permeating everything.

11—Essence Level

The eleventh level is a higher level of the sixth, or soul, body—primarily the "I Am-ness" area and the level at which we are in touch with our soul. When the sixth level has its vibrations raised to the eleventh level, the contact with one's eternal soul is clearer and deeper. One not only senses one's own essence better, but also better comprehends the essence of others.

12—Higher Divine Level

The twelfth level or body is the higher expression of the seventh level, which is a strong point of contact with the Divine. When the seventh level is permeated by the higher vibrations of the twelfth level, people will experience more oneness with God, the universe, and others, and have more God-like attributes.

Opening and Developing Bodies 8–12

The following is a meditation which can help raise one's vibrations to the higher levels. Areas of the body are given for the person to focus on as a means of contacting the levels easier.

Meditation 1: Combinations of Bodies

1. Sixth and First

Be aware of your sixth body, above your ears and where your neck curves into your shoulders. Be aware of your physical body, especially the arms and legs. Ask the sixth-level energies to come into the first level, refine them, lift it up so that it has the vibration of the sixth level. Have the sixth level and the first level become one but with the sixth-level energies predominating. Let the sixth level energy permeate your whole physical body.

2. Seventh and Second

Be aware of your crown chakra and your navel chakra. Bring the crown chakra energy into the navel. Use the seventh level into the second level to refine and uplift the emotional level. The emotional level is a lower octave of the divine. You cannot have a relationship with God through the mental level—it has to be at the feeling level, otherwise, you have nothing more than theology. You know *about* rather than *know*. Let the seventh-level energies permeate the second level.

3. Eighth and Third

To get in touch with the eighth level, focus on your breathing and imagine your breath, upon inhalation, going immediately out the breastbone and out the sides of your chest. Obviously, the air doesn't go out of the body that way, however, the prana does. This creates a powerful boost to mental energy which actually can affect all levels. Let the eighth-level energies permeate the third level. When doing this breathing, focus on your forehead and brain areas as they relate to the third level. Ask the energies of the eighth level to refine and lift up the energies of the third.

4. Ninth and Fourth

Focus on the top of your head and the bottom of your feet in order to get in touch with the ninth level. This level brings divine or heavenly information into the human level. Focus on bringing the energies of the ninth level into the heart area, as it is the entry point for the fourth level. Ask the energies of the ninth level to refine and uplift the energies of the fourth.

5. Tenth and Fifth

For the tenth level, you need to expand your consciousness way out around your body to where the energies are light and fine. Ask to be in touch with the tenth level. Bring that into the back—the point of entry for the fifth-level body. Ask the tenth-level energies to refine and uplift the fifth-level energies.

6. Eleventh and Sixth

For eleven, expand your consciousness even further out than you did for ten. Ask to be in touch with the eleventh level. Bring the energies of the eleventh level into the area above the head and where the sides of the neck come into your body. Ask eleventh-level energies to refine and uplift the sixth-level energies.

7. Twelfth and Seventh

Expand your consciousness even further out than for the eleventh level. Bring the energies of the twelfth level into the top of your head, which is the point of contact for the seventh level. Let these energies flood the seventh level to refine and uplift them. Afterwards you may want to remain in a quiet meditative state for ten or fifteen minutes. Some people prefer body movement first in order to further integrate the energies.

Beyond the Twelfth Level

It is also possible to explore the levels beyond twelve. Most people have some abilities on these higher levels, although they are not developed enough for sustained use. The following meditations will help put you in touch with these levels, and to see which ones feel familiar. It would be great to focus on those which do not feel easy or usable periodically in order to develop consciousness and abilities there. It's best to not overdevelop one area at the expense of an other. Balance is always best.

Meditation 2: Achieving Higher Levels

Refer to Chart 2.1 on page 24.

1. Start with the physical body. Become aware of your arms and legs and ask to really feel your body. Then ask its vibrations to lift to level six, hold for a few minutes, and then lift to level eleven and hold for a few minutes. Continue in the same way for the other numbers.

2. Do the emotional body, focusing on your navel and belly area in the beginning. Then continue with its higher numbers as you did with your physical body in Section 1.

   Do the mental body focusing on your forehead and brain area. Then continue with the higher numbers as you did in Section 1.

   Do the intuitional/compassionate body, focusing on your heart chakra in the beginning. Then continue with the higher numbers.

   Do the will/spirit body, focusing on your back in the beginning. Then continue with the higher numbers.

   Do the soul level body, focusing above the ears and sides of your neck where it curves into your body. Then continue with the higher numbers.

   Do the seventh level, focusing on the top of your head in the beginning. Then follow with meditating on the higher numbers.

Accessing Past and Future

We have been on our cycle of growth for thousands of lifetimes. Therefore, the spiral we are on has been going for some time. You may be on the top end of the spiral, or the low end of the spiral, or somewhere else in your growth.

We use 1 to 7 as basic numbers for our time. If we wish to access the past it is best to ask for a particular number of levels in the past. For instance, if you wish to explore past lives relevant to your physical body, you may ask for three levels back on the physical level or seven levels back, or whatever number you wish.

Meditation 3: Going into the Past

Be in a comfortable position, preferably lying down, so you have better concentration. Focus on your back and behind it.

Then ask to see a past life from (your choice) levels back, which corresponds to your physical body.

Relax in an aware state and watch the thoughts, feelings, and pictures that come to you. Meditate on any meanings for today.

This meditation may be done for any of the seven bodies. If you wish to access future lives, the following meditation may be helpful.

Meditation 4: Going into the Future

1. Be in a comfortable position, preferably lying down. Focus in front of your body (above if you are lying down).

2. Ask to see a future life when you will be functioning primarily on level (whatever you choose).

3. Be in a relaxed and aware state and watch what thoughts, feelings, and pictures come to you.

4. Meditate on any meanings for today.

Expanding Consciousness

Meditation is, of course, very vital in the process of expanding consciousness. However, if undirected, a person may go to the same levels over and over, thus developing some areas while ignoring others. This kind of development always slows down general growth because there isn't a balance. Dark areas in a person's consciousness develop as excess development on one level may deplete another.

Chart 2.2 gives information on body levels eight through twelve. By connecting with the level and then focusing on development through the listed nutrients the body level becomes more accessible to the person. Meditation on the properties, uses, and benefits will further expand the development of these body levels.

When you have worked with eight through twelve, it then becomes easier to open to the levels beyond twelve. The following is a meditation to help with levels beyond twelve.

Meditation 5: Beyond Levels

1. Be in a meditative state, open and relaxed.

2. Focus on the eighth level for a few minutes, then ask to be open to level thirteen.

3. When you feel you are in touch with level thirteen, you may ask any of the following:

    a. How could I connect with this level better?

    b. What nutrients will help in my development of this level?

    c. What are the properties for me on this level?

    d. What are the uses I might find for this level?

    e. What benefits will I receive from working with this level?

If you are not too exhausted, you may wish to repeat this with levels eighteen, twenty-three, and twenty-eight. This same meditation may be used for each of the body levels. However, it would be better not to do them all at once.

Body Level	Connecting Areas	Nutrients	Properties	Uses	Benefits
8	Eighth level breathing; feeling lighter	Orange color; faith; belief in higher power	Powerful mental abilities with Divine overtones	Miracles; transcending patterns and karma	Well-being, knowing you are not alone; effectiveness
9	Open ring around crown chakra and similar one in heels	Aqua color; expanded vision, conceptual abilities	As above, so below; bringing spiritual understanding to human levels	Seeing creativity already done on this level before you do it	Not having to work so hard
10	Expand consciousness beyond normal aura size to its lighter, finer vibrations	Blue color; love & energy from heart and back; willingness to receive	All-consuming love; forgiveness	The love covers a multitude of sins; part of the universe and easier to partipate in it	Feeling more a part of the universe and easier to partipate in it
11	Expand further than 10 to vibrations of 11	Purple color; compassion	Essence	More powerful than level 8; to know, change, heal creation	Become a partner with God in creation
12	Expand further than 11 to the vibration of 12	Radiant white; learning from experiencing suffering, depression	Divine, all-powerful, all-knowing	Blends inner and outer mystical levels	Become more Christ-like, more God-like

Chart 2.2 Developing Body Levels 8–12.

We need to learn what the properties, uses, and benefits are on these higher levels, as they will be quite different for each person. When even some what developed, the person will be able to contact a particular body level to help with matters relating to its area. The following is another meditation which can help general growth.

Meditation 6: Asking Questions

1. Choose a number of levels with which you wish to work.

2. Be in a meditative state.

3. Ask each level in turn if there is something you need to work out.

4. Or you may wish to ask the levels you've chosen to work with if there is a blessing or benefit waiting for you there.

Energy follows wherever you put your attention, so focusing on these areas periodically will automatically empower them. This will help you open to more genius-like abilities and insights. It is also interesting to know that whenever partially developed, these higher levels are filled with light.

It is not good to spend so much time on these higher levels that you ignore what needs to be done on the basic one through seven. Again, balance is important. Sometimes people who have achieved high levels as artists, inventors, researchers, or thinkers will seem to be unbalanced with total energies. It is though going off balance by overfocusing on one area improves what they do. However, some other part of their lives usually suffers. It may be in relationships, finances, or some other area. However, with the power of the newer astrological forces some focus is fine, but overall a person should have good balance. Spiritual growth especially requires good balance, so you don't become nutty or irrational.

Actually, when exploring these higher levels, many people may be surprised to find that some of them may be quite developed when others are not. This is an example of overfocus, which is fine in order to achieve something. You should then bring other areas up to the same level of proficiency.

Problem Solving

Many times things that seem like big problems are only that way because we are too close to them, or our vision is too narrow. If we can get to a higher level and get a broader perspective of the situation, not only can we adjust the amount of energy to devote to it, but many times we get the solution as well. We may also find that what we thought was a major problem is only a minor irritation. The following meditation may help.

Meditation 7: Problem Solving

1. Relax in a comfortable position, breathing peacefully.

2. Focus for a few minutes on what the problem is.

3. Focus also on your forehead and brain energy, so as to be in the mental, or third, level. Be aware of the problem from that level. Ask if there is a solution there.

4. Focus now on the eighth-level breathing (imagining the breath going out your breastbone and sides of your chest). Ask to be on the eighth level. Be aware of the problem. Ask if there is a solution there.

5. Let yourself feel light and open. Be aware of the area beyond your head. Ask your energies to be on the thirteenth level. Be aware of the problem. Ask if there is a solution there.

6. You may repeat with levels eighteen, twenty-three, and twenty-eight using the techniques from step 5.

If there aren't satisfactory answers, you may wish to work with other areas such as intuitional/compassionate or divine. Problems may include creative projects, work, or future careers. Physical problems may do better on the physical, or soul, level, while relationship concerns may do better on the emotional, intuitional/compassionate, will/spirit, or divine levels.

Sometimes you will get ideas for solutions on higher levels that may seem strange. Meditating on the solution can give you more information about why it could be helpful. It may just be that you have to expand your vision enough to include other directions. Sometimes your wishes and desires on the lower level have clouded or blocked the receiving of this higher information. Continued practice with these levels will make them very usable and you may find yourself going to these levels very easily, and sometimes automatically.

Relationships

Relationships are usually experienced most intensely on the lower levels. This often results in relating only in the physical, emotional, and mental ways. Opening to the higher levels automatically brings in a spiritual side not only to the physical, emotional, and mental levels, but also opens relationships to deeply meaningful spiritual areas.

It may be wise for individuals to check their higher levels for information before working with others on these levels. The following meditation can help explore higher levels.

Meditation 8: Relationship
Information from Emotional Levels

1. Focus on your navel and belly area so that you open to the second level, the emotional body.

2. While your attention is there, focus on a relationship you would like to understand better. Ask if

there is any information about the relationship at this level.

3. Expand your consciousness out in front of your navel/belly area. Ask to be on the seventh level. Ask if there is any in formation there.

4. Expand your consciousness further out and ask to be in touch with the twelfth level. Ask if there is any information there.

5. You may expand your consciousness further for the seventeenth, twenty-second, and twenty-seventh levels asking each if there is any information on these levels.

Meditation 9: Relationship Information on Intuitional/Compassionate and Will/Spirit Levels

The following directions may be used when focusing on the heart area for the intuitional/compassionate levels (4, 9, 14, 19, 24, and 29). For level nine be aware of the top of your head and the bottom of your feet. For succeeding levels expand your awareness beyond your head and feet.

You may do the same with the will/spirit levels (5, 10, 15, 25, and 30). This area may give you more information on the karmic interaction in the relationship. In fact, you may ask specifically, "What is the karma on this level?"

Meditation 10: Being on Higher Levels with a Friend

Begin by sitting comfortably facing a friend, breathing deeply and peacefully. Repeat the previous meditation from the intuitional/compassionate level.

Start with opening your heart areas and ask to be on level four. Ask what information is there. Share with each other.

Move to level nine by focusing on the top of your head and bottom of your feet. Ask to be in ninth-level energy. Ask if there is information there. Sometimes you may feel your spirits dancing above your head. Share with each other.

You may continue on the higher levels, fourteen through twenty-nine, each time being aware further out from your head and feet.

You may do the emotional and will/spirit levels using the techniques listed under emotional and will/spirit. It would, however, be good to have a rest before starting these.

Relationship with God

Since each person's primary relationship should be with God, or whatever they call the Divine Force, it would be excellent for spiritual as well as human growth to work on this area. Your relationship with God is so individual and unique—don't be surprised by what you find in the various levels.

It is also interesting to note that people who reject a divine source quite often don't believe in themselves well either. In other words, if their concept of God or a higher power is small, their concepts of them selves may be small, too. Sometimes this smallness reverberates into large egos.

Meditation 11: Relating with God

1. Focus on the top of your head and ask to be in touch with the seventh level. Ask what your relationship with God is from this level.

2. Expand your consciousness beyond your head and ask to be on the twelfth level. Ask what your relationship with God is from this level.

3. You may continue to expand your consciousness further out above your head for each of levels 12, 17, 22, 27, and 32.

Pets, Plants, and Nature

In the coming years, more people will develop closer and much more aware relationships with their pets. We will become closer to plants and the rest of nature, too.

Meditation 12: Pets and Plants

One may follow the above patterns using the emotional body, extending energy out in front and using levels 2, 7, 12, 17, 22, and 27. An alternate is to use the soul level and expand around the entire body using the numbers 6, 11, 16, 21, 26, and 31. Ask to be in touch with pets or plants.

Meditation 13: Nature

Using the divine level (7, 12, 17, 22, 27, and 32) and asking for oneness with nature and the universe is meaningful as well. Extend your consciousness above your head for this one.

Be careful not to overdo these meditations as they can bring in very powerful energies, and can make you irritable or nervous. If that happens, it's best not to do them for a while. Another possible concern is that you may trigger a kundalini release and it would need to be attended to.*

---

*If this happens, we refer you to *Kundalini and the Chakras* by Genevieve Lewis Paulson.

You will find that you are being pulled to develop these areas, however, and it is much easier if you consciously open to them. If you wish to go beyond the levels we've given, by all means do so. However, it is best in the beginning to concentrate on the ones listed. Some may wish to work only on the first three levels in the beginning. Do what is comfortable for you. We wish you great success as you explore your infinite potential. Our evolution is definitely being accelerated and we are in for quite a ride.

Chapter 3

Formation
of the
Bodies

LIFE DOES NOT have a begin-
ning or an end; it is part of a cycle. The top of the cycle is
in the spiritual realm. When we are on the spiritual level,
we review past lives and with the help of guides plan our
next incarnation. Decisions may include any known
karma to be absolved, additional lessons to learn for our
spiritual growth, what type of body would best facilitate
this growth, what type of parents would give the greatest
help, and what birth chart would give the optimum
chance for success in accomplishing our "life goals."

When these decisions are made, we then aim for a
conception time that is best suited for these purposes.
This becomes very tricky because we are depending on
others, beyond our reach, to be cooperative.

The forming of the bodies can begin before or after conception depending on the time constraints of the soul. Most of us go in and out of the body, working with its development. However, total entry into the new body can be at conception or any time up to birth—it all depends on the scheduling needs of the individual.

If a soul has built up a lot of karma and needs to absolve it quickly in order to get back to spiritual progress, that soul may plan several lifetimes in advance. They may be short but intense lives, and the soul may skip right from death in one to the birth of the next with little or no preparation time in between. This can create a situation where the soul may have to accept a body that doesn't completely meet its needs, but was the only one available at the time. This would make this person's life even more challenging. At other times, an individual may spend hundreds of years in between lives. Growth does continue in an unincarnated state, however it is greatly accelerated when done in a physical form. When the soul begins the forming of the bodies, the first is the mental body.

There are entities for whom the mental level is home, as they work to assist us in the forming of our mental bodies according to our soul's plan. They gather the "new mental material" needed and help us select from our own "old mental material" in the forming of our next mental body. New mental matter is "unimpressed." It contains no predetermined thought forms, like a blank tape or computer disk. It is there to be used as needed. Old mental matter is impressed with thoughts, ideas, and concepts from previous lives. This matter cannot be taken beyond the mental into spiritual realms so it is left behind as a "personal inventory," to be reused whenever we return for another incarnation.

Our personal inventory can contain talents, traits, tendencies, and karma of past lives. We choose this material as needed to best give us the opportunity to absolve old karmic debts, and prevent creating new ones in the next life. As long as we have negatively impressed material we must return to deal with it. Sometimes information from the personal inventory becomes a drive, or force, to help in the new life. When we have an area of little or no experience, it generally turns negative and can only become positive with greater levels of experience. When we no longer have negatively impressed material on any level, we have no need to return to the physical life and then might return only to assist others. When we have completely assembled the mental body of our new life, we then move on to the emotional body. The process is the same, guided by the entities of the emotional level, and we assemble the new unimpressed emotional matter and the old impressed emotional matter that contains our feelings, fears, pleasures, and karma from previous lives to be used or absolved in the new life.

When these higher bodies are formed we are ready for entry into the physical body (including its etheric level). Our biological parents are the guides for the formation of the physical body, and our guardian parents (they may or may not be biological parents) are the guides for the nurturing of that physical body. The talents, traits, tendencies, feelings, fears, pleasures, pain, and karma or impressed physical matter is genetic. It contains the genetic impression of our ancestors (some of whom may be ourselves), which we choose according to our needs and challenges for this life.

Some of the physical influences can be from our own past lives. For them to come through physically would indicate the power or strength of that event on us. For example, we might be born with a birthmark or a deformity in a place where a mortal wound had been suffered in a previous incarnation. During our physical existence there are many situations that arise, many of them predestined. These events are placed in our life and planned for by us. We program them to give us the opportunity to deal with them expressly for the fulfillment of karma or to enable us to make spiritual progress. They are generally changes of a negative nature, which give us the task of growing and learning how to make them positive. Sometimes they are positive and the challenge is to keep them that way. How we deal with these events determines future karma and spiritual growth. If we don't handle it well enough, we may have to do it again. If we do handle the event properly, not only is karma absolved, but now we have a skill and experience for handling similar situations. When we reach the end of our physical life, we leave our physical bodies behind. Any evolutionary changes that are left go into the group consciousness and is also left in our sons and daughters for their edification. The learning and growth, impressed on our physical beings, is passed on genetically. The race evolves and grows based on our accumulated efforts.

When we leave the physical realm at death, we enter the emotional (astral) world. Here we review our life to determine successes and failures. The successes become our assets, and the failures become our challenges in a future life. We then begin the process of shedding the emotional body. This is done with detachment. If there is something we feel strongly about, that attachment can keep us locked in this place for a very long time. Some beings feel that this is heaven because they can have whatever they want, but it is this want that locks them here, and keeps them from attaining higher levels. There are other areas that feel like hell because of being so totally immersed in their own negative feelings and attitudes. At some point desire fades, we become detached and let go, thus releasing ourselves for the next level. The emotional matter we had during this life is left behind, impressed with our assets and challenges, waiting for our return in the next life.

We then enter the mental level, where we review our mental life during this incarnation, again examining our assets and challenges acquired during this life. Here, also, being locked into an idea or concept can trap us on this level until we can learn open-mindedness or a detachment from ideas and concepts. As we let go of our favorite thoughts, the mental matter that is impressed with the ideas from our life is left behind, storing our assets and challenges for whenever we return in a future incarnation. We now re-enter the spirit world, where we re-examine the totality of this life and make plans for the next. When we reach a certain level of individual evolution, we can break free from this cycle of birth, death, and rebirth, and continue up the ladder of spiritual bodies to oneness with God. The following are some meditations to help explore the above information.

Meditation 1: Exploring the Makeup of the Bodies

Kundalini is a powerful evolutionary energy, which helps raise our consciousness. It is active in everyone at all times, which can be called upon to help in meditations or other pursuits. For this exercise we recommend you ask for the kundalini currently available to you to help you in the exercise.*

1. **Physical Body:** Be aware of your arms and legs as points of contact for the physical body. Ask to be in touch with your physical body.

    a. Ask the available kundalini to fill your the body, to help expand your consciousness.

    b. Observe your physical body. Look at and feel its structure.

    c. Ask to see how it was formed for this life.

    d. Ask what thought forms were included at that time. It could include talents, karma, purpose, desires, hindrances, as well as a number of other things. Be open to what the possibilities are.

    e. Ask which of these thought forms are active in your life at this time.

---

*If you wish further information on kundalini, please refer to *Kundalini and the Chakras* by Genevieve Lewis Paulson.

f. Ask to see what other energies are available that you are not using at this time.

g. Ask how you could better use the assets available.

2. **Emotional Body (Astral):** Be in touch with your navel and belly area as points of contact. Ask to be in touch with your emotional body. Then follow the instructions listed under step A.

3. **Mental Body:** Be in touch with your forehead and brain area as points of contact. Ask to be in touch with your mental body. Then follow the instructions listed under step A.

4. **Intuitional/Compassionate Body:** Be in touch with the center of your chest and heart area. Ask to be in touch with your intuitional/compassionate body. Then follow the instructions listed under step A.

5. **Will/Spirit Body:** Be in touch with your back and the back of your heels. Ask to be in touch with your will/spirit body. Then follow instructions listed under step A.

6. **Soul Level Body:** Be in touch with the top of your forehead in the center, just below the hairline and around the outside of your body. Ask to be in touch with the soul level body. Then follow instructions listed under step A.

7. **Divine Level Body:** Be in touch with the top of your head. Ask to be in touch with your divine level body. Then follow instructions listed under step A.

Life Choices

After a person has completed much or all of the karma allotted to this life to be worked out, and has completed much or all of the projects and learning planned for this life, as well as developed qualities which were planned to achieve this life, boredom or a sense of uselessness may occur. You may feel without a sense of direction. When this happens and one's lifespan has not reached its end, it is time to set new goals and find new things to learn. Sometimes you may become ill trying to understand the change happening to you.

A time-out is very important, whether one does it in illness, through a vacation, or by making space for oneself. Being open in a meditative way, reading, and exploring options are all important ways to help determine new goals that may give a person a new direction. The following are several meditations that can help a person discover if it is time to take a new direction.

Meditation 2: New Directions

1. Let yourself be in a daydreaming state, with a feeling of floating. Visualize yourself being in occupations you have thought about, being creative in new ways, or opening to some totally new field. Let your daydreams take you where they will. Even if you program the daydream in the beginning, and, if you let it unfold, quite often you will find it changes course and brings you new information. Don't reject anything right away. Give the new information time to process itself in your system.

2. If you like what comes through to you, feel the new ideas or information in your body and see if it resonates with you. That will help it manifest. Otherwise, daydream energy can dissipate on its own.

Meditation 3: New Directions from the Bodies

1. Go through the bodies listed in the previous section, asking each body, in turn, what other things

were in your storehouse when your bodies were formed. Sometimes the desire came through, but not the drive, because other things took precedence. When the other things are completed, perhaps the drive will now be available.

2. Make a list of ideas and information you receive and, at a later date, see which seem important and possible for you.

The energies of evolution seem so much stronger and faster that it is much easier to complete one's life tasks early. Sometimes it is as though a person has lived three or four lifetimes in one body. It is really exciting to think that so much can be accomplished with one body. Also when people look forward to other things that can be done, there is preparation for things that can help in the next life.

Chapter 4

Auras
and
Bodies

WE ARE COMPOSED of much more than what physically shows. We have incredible energy patterns throughout our bodies, and some of them expand beyond the physical body. This expanded energy pattern is called an aura and it fills what is called "the auric field." People with lots of energy will have stronger and larger auric fields. In Bishop Leadbeater's book *Man Visible and Invisible,* he shows the auras as contained within the etheric web. It has been our experience that, unless the person has little development or energy, the astral, mental and spiritual auras can all go beyond the confines of the etheric web.

A window can let in light, however, if it is open and then all sorts of things can come in: rain, snow, wind, birds, insects, or whatever comes that way. It is similar

Figure 4.1 Etheric Body Aura

with the web. When it is in its regular state, it allows some movement in and out. However, if there are holes in it, all sorts of things can come in, especially negativity.

These auras reflect the condition of the particular bodies each person has. A very developed person will have spiritual auras which expand miles around the body. Their presence will be felt in a large area. Great teachers and leaders will have spiritual auric fields which will help those in their presence learn and develop. On the opposite side, if you have much negativity or depression in your system and aura that, too, will affect those near you. However, the effect is adverse.

Humans have auras; physical, etheric (higher physical), emotional, mental, and spiritual. They interpenetrate one another and a person needs to change focus according to which aura is being viewed. It is important to learn more about this area of our lives so as to give us better choices for well-being and development.

Viewing or Sensing Auras and Bodies

Through meditation, many people develop the ability to see not only energy around other people, but also around trees, plants, rocks, and other objects. These auras reflect the energy pattern prevalent in the system; sometimes the aura is in color, sometimes as pure energy and, occasionally, some will sense, or *feel,* the aura. It will appear more as a mist than a solid color.

Physical Body Aura

This aura extends about four inches out around the body, and doesn't appear to change much. It is more "solid" in much of the same way the physical body is. The other auras are more changeable according to health, moods, and attitudes.

Etheric Body Aura

The etheric body is the higher form of the physical body. It shows as a bluish or grayish purple line about one-eighth to one-quarter inch around a person. It is sometimes called the etheric double since it is the same shape (only slightly larger) than the physical body.

Its aura consists of two parts. One is a band of white about one-and-a-half inches thick (see Figure 4.1, opposite page). This band of white relates to a person's vitality and, if it is much more than an inch wide, it signifies that the person's vitality is "leaking" out into the aura. Those with the wider bands are usually very tired or depressed. Vitality of this aura is represented by the brilliance of the white band.

The other part of this aura consists of narrow energy streams going out from the body (Figure 4.2). If a person is depressed or

Figure 4.2   Healthy Etheric Lines

Figure 4.3   Depressed or Nervous Person's Etheric Energy

Figure 4.4   Uptight or Nervous Person's Etheric Energy

ill the energy streams may go down (Figure 4.3). If a person is uptight or nervous, the energy will go up (Figure 4.4).

You may wish to imagine your energy streams going straight out, then down, then up, and finish with straight out. When these energy streams are straight out, they protect the etheric double and the nerves. They also help sense information. This aura may go out about sixteen inches from a person's body.

Emotional Body Aura

The part of our system relating to emotions, feelings, and motivations has its own vibratory system, which may be called a body. It is only seen through its aura which is the color manifestation of its energy. The aura of a person whose emotional body is more developed is shown in Plate 1a; a person with less development is shown in Plate 1b (see color plate section).

It is possible to change the aura coloring immediately by changing your emotions. However, it is more difficult to change the *brilliance* and *definition* of colors, as that has to do with your overall development. The more developed the person, the lighter and more brilliant the colors will be. Muddy, less defined colors characterize a less developed emotional body.

The emotional aura may extend about thirty-six inches from the physical body. If a person is very emotional, it may extend four or five feet. However, this usually makes other people very uncomfortable, because it affects their auras in the same negative way, or, even if positive, still can have an adverse effect, by wiping a person out with its intensity. A balanced peacefulness is best.

The emotional body's aura colors will show as a person's energy changes, sometimes very quickly. Anger will show as a jagged, dark-red streak, or there may appear to be storm centers of darkish colors swirling around their body. The color shadings can change the meanings, so it is best to learn to feel the colors and thus determine the particular meaning. These are some other colors which may be seen in the emotional body aura along with possible interpretations:

Bright Pink: Creative plans.

Pale Rose: Unselfish affection.

Red: Can be all sorts of things. Clear red tends to be available energy. Darker red mixed with black can be anger. Darker reds mixed with brown can be pure lust.

Orange: Intensity. It may be an important healing color of the New Age, although most people aren't quite ready for orange as a healing color yet. Many people don't like the color orange. They find it uncomfortable to look at, and too intense. Orange relates to power. If a person doesn't deal well with his or her own power, then that intensity can become very uncomfortable.

Gold: Healing color.

Muddy Yellow: Heavy, unproductive thinking.

Yellow: Indicates higher intellectual power.

Very Light Yellow: Highest intellect.

Apple Green: Sympathy, healing.

Forest or Grass Green: The green of growth.

Green with Black: Jealousy.

Blue: Devotion or wisdom.

Navy Blue: Usually means fanaticism.

Luminous Lilac Blue: Higher spirituality.

Lavender: Healing, spiritual, being in tune.

Purple: Can mean authority, or just being plain pushy.

Brown: Mixed with other colors it is not good, and shows anger, fear, and lust. By itself, it is indicative of strong grounding and may be somewhat protective.

Copper: Earthly spirituality, alertness.

Gray: Some people feel that gray is a spiritual color. However, it seems logical that it would have to be the mother-of-pearl type gray, instead of a dingy gray. Darker grays usually mean exhaustion or depression.

White: Spirituality.

Mental Body Aura

The mental aura relates to the mental body. Again, this is only an energy manifestation. The body energies beyond physical do not have a solid shape, as in the physical body. The mental aura is much stronger around the head area and more so in a developed person (see Plates 2a and 2b). The mental aura doesn't change as quickly as the emotional aura, and more directly relates to the overall life development rather than the moment as does the emotional aura.

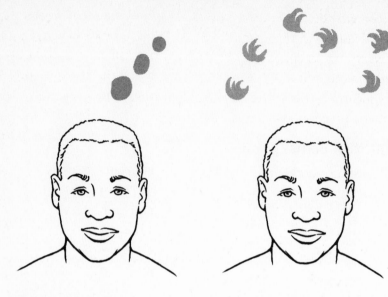

Figure 4.5   Prayer Energy
Sent Out to Another

Figure 4.6   Obsessive
Thoughts Curling Back

Figure 4.7   Strong Concept

Figure 4.8   Thought Replica

Geometric shapes (relating to thought forms) may show in this aura (see Figures 4.5 through 4.8, at left). This aura may extend about seventy-two inches from the physical body. It interpenetrates the other auras and is not easily seen. However, if the person is primarily mentally oriented, it may be stronger and more visible than the etheric or emotional auras.

Spiritual Bodies Aura

This is the most beautiful of the auras and relates more to the overall development through a person's lives. Change here is slower than the etheric, emotional, and mental auras. However, this growth stays with a person all their lives. This aura may extend for miles, or the person may be able to project it even further.

Some people develop very strong on one path, or it may be said, on one color ray (see Plate 3). They will have achieved high energy development in one area or another, manifesting as one predominant color.

The colors are simply visual manifestations of particular energies we use to intensify our development or service. The person who is fully able to work with the major colors will have a most beautiful colorful aura (see Plate 14). It will be vibrant and well-defined. It will extend a great distance from the person. It is difficult to see for two reasons: (1), You need to view it from a highly developed state, and (2), very few people have developed this far.

Auras from Inner Levels

These auras relate to the inner bodies and are connected to the inner world. They will have darker colors, and the white light will appear silver. We are not dealing with these auras in this book since they are very difficult to see unless one has developed inner sight.

Enhancing Auras

Many things will enhance or expand the aura. Affection and hugging activate these energies. Being happy, inspired, ecstatic, all

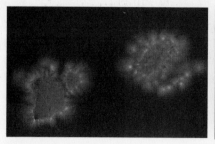 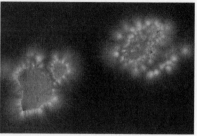

Figure 4.9 Iron Pyrite aura   **Figure 4.10** Iron Pyrite aura
enhanced by human aura

these increase the vitality, brighten the colors, and expand the auras.

When you hold a rock or mineral, or are close to one that resonates with you, then both the rock's aura (see Figures 4.9 and 4.10, above) and yours will brighten and expand.

Closing Auras

If you feel you are ever in an unsafe situation, or are around negative people, then your aura will pull in, thus closing it off for protection. Living primarily with a protected aura slows down your development, openness, ability to relate to others, and your spiritual or creative expression. In safe situations and away from negative people, you need to open your aura again. This can be done by breathing deeply and imagining your auric energy expanding until you feel comfortable.

Seeing Auras

There are several techniques to help in seeing auras. Don't give up if it doesn't work immediately. It is learning a new way of sight, and may take a while for you to get the feel of it.

Meditation 1: Seeing Auras

1. Have someone stand or sit in front of a light-colored or white wall with no shadows on it.

2. Focus your attention on the person's forehead, and allow colors to come into your peripheral vision. It is very difficult to look directly at an aura and see it until you have progressed in this ability.

3. As you look at the person focus your vision about one foot in front or one foot behind them. This helps your eyes to unfocus so the colors may appear.

4. Open up the area around your navel (emotional chakra) as this helps open you to the astral level, making it easier to view the astral aura.

5. Watch people who are public speakers. Usually they are in a much stronger energy pattern than normal, and the colors around them will be more vivid. It is all right to stare at a speaker. In fact, he or she will think that you are paying attention.

6. It is difficult to see your own aura, but if you will sit in front of a mirror with a light behind you (not casting shadows or showing directly into the mirror), it is possible. You may use either step 1, 2, and 3 to help. Being in a meditative state will help power your aura.

Although auras surround the entire body, the most developed part is usually around the head/shoulders area (as shown in Plates 1a through 15). These figures show various auras of less and more developed persons.

Developing Your Auras

Our growth automatically improves our auras since they are a reflection of what is in us. However, we can work specifically with the auras as a way of increasing overall growth. The following are some meditations that can help in aura development.

Meditation 2: General Aura Development

Relax in a comfortable position.

1. One at a time, fill yourself with the primary and secondary colors (red, orange, yellow, green, blue, and purple). If you can't see the colors, just imagine them. After feeling them in your body, expand them to about ten feet around your body so that your auras are more strongly affected. After going through the colors, fill yourself with a radiant light, and then extend it out beyond your body. Try to extend the radiance as far as you can from your body and still maintain awareness of it. If the colors are luminous or radiant, they indicate higher spiritual development. Muddy, dark colors indicate not much development, or the person is temporarily in a very bad mood.

2. Do the above exercise again, this time using the tertiary colors (coral, gold, yellow/green, aqua, lilac, and red-violet).

3. Fill your body and then the auric space with the energy of qualities, one at a time. You may wish to use love, gentleness, enlightened peace (more active and lighter than peace), patience, and strength. You may have other qualities you would like to use.

Meditation 3: Strengthening the Aura

Stand in the middle of the room and breathe into your auric energy. Try to expand it to all areas of the room. This will help you strengthen your aura so that you become aware of other people's energies at the edge of your aura rather that have them penetrate your body area. If you let others' energies into your system, you may pick up whatever others are feeling. Usually negative feelings are the easiest to pick up from others.

Meditation 4: Strengthening the Etheric Double Aura

1. Stand and feel the energy around your body.

2. Ask to feel the etheric aura. Feel your energies going straight out. Imagine you are breathing in and out of the energies for a few minutes.

Meditation 5: Strengthening the Emotional Aura

Ask to feel your emotional aura (this is the one most easily affected by others). Breathe into it for a few minutes and fill it with calm, peace, and vibrancy. The vibrancy brings a sense of aliveness.

Meditation 6: Clearing and Strengthening the Mental Aura

Ask to feel the mental aura. Is it crowded with thought forms? Breathe into it for a few minutes, asking that all unnecessary or unwanted thought forms dissipate.

If other thought forms remain, you may ask what
they have to tell you. Fill them with light yellow and a
light vibrant orange. Breathe into them.

An awareness of the auras can give them more strength, and
thus more protection for you.

Development of the Spiritual Aura

The spiritual aura brings development of past lives into the present. Each life we add something to this aura, whether it be development of spiritual qualities or overall spiritual presence. When a
person focuses on this aura with intent, not only will the already
accrued development become more usable, but also new growth
will be enhanced.

Meditation 7: Qualities in the Spiritual Aura

Ask to feel your spiritual aura. Breathe into it for a few
minutes. What spiritual qualities do you sense you have
developed?

In Plate 14, the aura shows a highly developed person who has
focused on the function of bringing spiritual truths into human
understanding. (Note the large amount of aqua and yellow/green
shades.) Other examples are:

A person focusing on love would have **rose** and **rosy-
gold** predominant in the aura.

One who focuses on healing would have **gold** as a predominant color.

One who focuses on *samadhi*, or oneness with God,
would have **lavender**, or **lilac**, predominant color.

One who focuses on development would show **yel-low/green** predominantly.

Red-violet would be the predominant color in a person with a strong will devoted to the divine plan.

The above colors are tertiary colors formed by combining primary and secondary colors. (For further information on tertiary colors see the author's book *Energy-Focused Meditation*.)

Meditation 8: Development of the Spiritual Aura

Ask to be in touch with your spiritual aura, then fill it with the tertiary colors one at a time (rosy-gold, gold, yellow/green, aqua, lilac, and red-violet). The strongest color would be the one you have developed most or are currently working on. Try to have some sense of all the colors in order to help speed your overall growth.

Someone who hasn't reached full development (see Plate 3) will need the intensity and vibrations of a particular tertiary color to achieve what is needed to complete or balance growth. This shows their current destiny path.

A fully developed person (see Plate 14) will have the primary and secondary colors, which will be more evenly distributed because of the development of all levels. However, you will note that the further out the aura extends, the larger the colored sections. The colors will be pastel because the person's aura is moving back into the source of the color—pure light.

The aura will have clear or translucent white columns, which form spokes in a slightly egg shaped cosmic wheel around the person. Sometimes the columns have a slight golden color rather than translucent white.

Meditation 9: Spokes and
Wheel of the Developed Aura

Imagine the twelve spokes and wheel of the developed aura around you. Fill it with all the colors as shown in Plate 14. Let the energies be vibrant and alive. This helps to center and raise your vibrations. If you feel crabby or restless afterwards, take it easy on this exercise until later when you have adjusted to the force of these energies better. The mystic will have vibrant, iridescent, or fire-like colors. Tertiary shadings may be apparent between the other colors.

Thought Forms

In its natural state, the auric field is calm and gives a person a feeling of well-being. If there is negative energy, or thought forms coming from others, or a person is generating them him or herself, the aura will be distorted or disturbed; thus creating confusion or a feeling of being distraught. Thought forms (Figures 4.5 through 4.8, page 56) are energy masses caused by strong thoughts residing in the aura until they are recognized, used, or dissipated. They may be from the person's own thoughts, or they may come from others. Any time you have a strong thought, positive or negative, about someone, it will go to them and, if negative, will distort his or her aura.

However, if the person has a strong aura it will tend to bounce the thought form back to the sender, sometimes letting the sender know that the thought form was unwelcome. At times it may instead bounce off to another person connected to the receiver, thus someone may receive very negative energies not intended for her or him.

Thought forms are also caused by extreme worry about someone or something. If you have a problem or concern you don't wish to deal with and "put it out of your mind," it will usually linger in your aura. Persons who are able to read auras can sometimes see

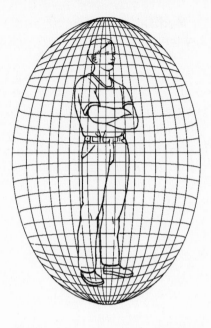

Figure 4.11 The Etheric Web

and comprehend the source of these thought forms. If there is enough of them or if they are sufficiently negative, it will distort the energy around the aura and cause upsetting feelings to the receiver.

The Protective Web

In addition to the auras mentioned we also have a luminous web of energy around us in the shape of an egg (see Figure 4.11). This web (sometimes called "the etheric web") protects us from strong cosmic energies until we are developed enough to use them. If there are any holes in a person's web, they may be subject to such strong energies that one cannot use them, and they turn negative. Negative forces also can come in these holes (see Figure 4.12, next page).

Strong anger outbursts are the most usual method of creating holes. Psychic attacks or negative energies may penetrate the auric field, or even create holes in the web.

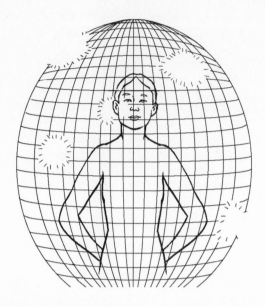

Figure 4.12　Holes in the Etheric Web

Meditation 10: Repairing the Web

1. If you feel out of sorts, distraught, or confused, surround yourself with an ultraviolet shield. You cannot see it, but your body knows it's there. If the disruptive energies are coming from someone else they will leave. You may see the sender's face or think of him when you do this. If so, just send blessings to him. He may be having a hard day.

2. Fill the area around you with love and blessings. This will help modify what comes to you, and what you send out!

3. Check your etheric web. Do you feel holes or open spaces? (refer to Figure 4.12.) If so, visualize any negative energy going back out the hole. Then imagine or visualize the hole coming together to

close it. Send extra energy to reinforce the hole. You will know you have done this if you feel better. You can achieve a lot with strong thoughts.

4. Ask if the hole or disturbance is caused by a past life that you need to deal with. To do this, focus your energy on where the hole was, let yourself be in a reverie state and see what information comes. A hole in the web may also be caused by strong cosmic or spiritual energy trying to come in to you with information. Focusing on the area and being in a reverie state can help you determine what actually did cause it.

Varieties of Auras

Plates 4 through 15 show a variety of auras (see color insert). Each person's aura will vary somewhat with his or her moods because their combinations of energies will be different.

Importance of the Aura

Much work is being done these days to heal and strengthen the physical body and to develop other areas through growth and meditation. It is time now to seriously consider the auric field as a part of our total package, and to work with development of this important space. We hope this chapter has given you some insights and practices to help in your overall development.

Chapter 5

The Seven Senses

OUR SENSES ARE very important to our development. It's through the senses that we experience events and interactions. The senses help us to know the essence of things and discern our relationship to them. Without our senses, growth would be difficult. When one sense is gone, such as eyesight, another sense usually becomes stronger. However, if a person chooses consciously, or unconsciously, to shut off a sense, sometimes others close down, too. When one chooses not to develop or use certain senses, then it does slow down the availability or richness of the total experience. As we develop in our spiritual growth, our senses begin to open more on their own. Purposely working for the development of the sensor capacity of the senses and using them can, in turn, speed growth.

The senses are sometimes seen as paths to negativity if the person uses them extensively for sensual purposes. When the senses are developed to higher levels their purposes become somewhat blurred to distinction, and one becomes more synesthetic. For instance, something may "feel" delicious or we may hear something that "sounds" like velvet. Anything that happens to us registers on *all* the sensual levels, however many times we are only aware of a few of the levels. Usually, the stronger the experience, the more the information from the senses are recognized.

In some spiritual or peak experiences, we may be aware of information from all the senses. Some years ago, when I was in my sixties, I had planned to sleep in a tent on a mountaintop. Since the temperature fell to the low twenties that night, and the tent had no heat, it seemed stupid, to say the least. However, when I left my truck and started for the tent I started to hear celestial music. I stopped and realized I was being shown the notes as they sounded, too. Then my body felt touched by them. I was aware that the air smelled fresh and crisp. My instinctual and knowing levels opened to me and a deep but exciting peace came over me. I knew I was doing the right thing. I had not been thinking about the uses of all the senses at the time or I would have stuck my tongue out and tasted the air.

I slept two winters in the tent and two more in an unheated cabin. This forced me into developing the use of tumo (psychic heat), as well as other abilities gained through this adventure. Many times we choose, or are forced into, situations which push our growth. We may not realize all we have gained in our experiences until later.

The seven senses are:

- sight

- hearing

- touch

- smell

- taste
- instinct
- knowing

Senses as Value Sensors

One of the senses' functions, or even of all the senses, is to let us know if situations are safe or if an object has value for us or person would be harmful to us or if the object or person needs to be avoided. For instance, on the instinctual level you may sense that a person means to do you harm, and should not be trusted. If you are using both the instinctual and knowing levels, the message may be that the person *does* mean harm, but that you can avoid the harm by certain interactions and still have a relationship. Or the knowing level may accentuate the instinctual level information and bring information on how to change your course of interaction so as not to be involved with the particular person.

In another example, an apple may be beautiful, taste and smell great, but be of no particular value to you at the time if your value sensor tells you that you are not hungry. The sense of value would not be important. At another time, when you are hungry and you looked at the apple, your value sensor from the instinctual level would tell you to eat it. All our senses are part of every experience whether or not we are aware of them. Expanding one's awareness of the senses can bring in more information and sense of value.

Prism Effect

An event or experience has a prism effect and in order to more fully develop your awareness and ability to use the effects, practice is necessary. Imagine how a prism works. White light is refracted into many different colors. In much the same way, an event or experience refracts into the separate elements of instinct, touch, taste, smell, hearing, seeing, and knowing.

Meditation 1: Experiencing the Prism Effect

Think of a recent event, or a powerful one from earlier in life.

Feel the event in your body, which becomes the prism for the experience. Especially focus on the area behind your solar plexus and about one-and-a-half inches above it (behind the xiphoid process).

Breathe into this area and feel the energy of the event. Let the event come as fully as possible into your consciousness.

1. What did you *see?*

2. What did you *hear?*

3. What did you *feel?*

4. What did you *smell?*

5. What did you *taste?*

6. Focusing on your navel, as well as your abdominal area, what did your *instincts* tell you?

7. Expanding further into the area behind the xiphoid process, was there a "knowing" that gave you information about the purpose of the event for you?

If you received information from four or five areas, you did well. You may wish to review it at a later date, in case more information comes through. All of your senses would have had some reaction to the event, even if your awareness couldn't pull it through.

In this kind of exercise, it is possible to get the bigger picture of events or experiences, thus giving you greater choices for actions and reactions. This kind of exercise increases your ability to use your senses as value sensors. Another benefit from experiencing all of the senses, besides information, is that your system feels nourished from the more complete awareness.

Problems with Development

If some or many of your senses are not operating well, value sensors can indicate negative things to you in a variety of ways. You may turn up the corners of your nose, feel nauseated, or feel crawly or prickly sensations on your skin. Sometimes you may feel as though you should leave and area, and don't know why at the time. It's a good idea to learn your body's way of trying to alert you to unpleasant or dangerous situations.

If a person is rigid, judgmental, insecure, or closed, the use of the instinctual and knowing senses are usually very slow to respond in clear ways. They may be trained to follow the negative patterns instead and thus give an incorrect report. Some people are afraid of some of the senses, especially feeling (touch). It can be scary to feel on deep levels. Sometimes sexuality is the only way some people allow themselves to feel deeply. However, to completely experience the senses, especially feeling on deep levels, is a way to release blocks, which in turn opens energy flows. This allows you to feel more alive and aware.

Exploring the Senses

We use our senses all day, every day, in a variety of ways. When our awareness increases, we automatically get greater use of them. The following is some information to help foster your awareness.

Smell

We often underestimate smell and how it can affect us in positive ways. Sometimes we focus on one smell, such as incense or perfume, so much we don't experience other levels of smell. Our sources of positive, life-enhancing smells should be changed periodically in order to experience greater vibrations through this sense. Some people grow gardens with many distinctly perfumed flowers. This is a great way to extend the opportunity for positive smells. When it is a beautiful smell it is usually referred to as "essence" or "perfume." However, if it is a bad smell it is usually referred to as an "odor."

Our pursuit to eliminate bad odors is in itself pretty strong. Stores carry quite an array of deodorizers for rooms, cars, pets, and humans. We do not seem to be able to tolerate unpleasant odors. Bad odors can and do bring us into a more negative space. There is a very positive side to bad smells, however, because they can warn us of danger or that food has spoiled.

Many phrases demonstrate other ways of using our noses. "Nose for news," "smell trouble," "turn up one's nose," and "things just don't smell right" are a few.

On higher levels some people are able to smell their own soul essence, or that of others, or even the essence of guides and angels. These smells are around us even though our sensitivity may not be fully developed enough to recognize them.

Taste

Taste is not just a word for food. We even use the phrase that people are "tasteless" or have "bad" taste in reference to their clothing, how they act, or how they decorate their homes. If we like it, we say he or she has "good taste." Our senses have become part of our language well beyond their basic meaning.

Our sensation of taste with food is dependent largely on our ability to smell. It is possible, however, that as we develop greater sense awareness, new tastes will develop beyond the four we now have, which include sweet, sour, bitter, and salty.

Touch and Feeling

Touching also applies to the emotional and spiritual experiences where one is "deeply touched." The vibrations of some experiences have been so strong that we literally feel the *touch* of the energy. It also usually implies we were somehow changed by the experience. Some people are so hard-hearted that vibrations of this type rarely get through. They are untouched by what happens. On the other hand, some people report God has touched their lives and made a difference.

We need a variety of things to touch in our lives. Plants, animals, soft clothing, leather, all bring energy to us. The greatest, however, is the touch of another human in kindness and love. Many years ago a friend of mine was caring for her aged mother. In her mother's last years she was bedridden, blind, and deaf. The woman, in her younger days, had enjoyed gardening and being outdoors. Her daughter would, when the seasons changed, bring some indication of that to her mother: a handful of snow, a daffodil, and other garden items and help her mother hold them in her hands and experience the changes. Many times, through that woman's life, these things had meaning and now they still were for her a connection to life.

Hearing

We also use hearing differently from its basic meaning. When we understand someone, we say, "I hear you," or, "I really heard that." It then becomes something that we comprehend on deeper levels.

Our ears are bombarded by the vibrations of different sounds. Sometimes we block out certain ranges of vibrations unconsciously. Some of us get into the habit consciously of tuning out certain sounds or people. If we want to tune something or someone out, that may not be bad. What *is* bad, however, is when the areas are left closed off for periods of time and our ability to hear diminishes. We need to learn to tune back in when things can be handled better. We need to plan times to hear music, the sounds of nature, or other vibrations as a way of resting or uplifting ourselves. Consciously taking charge of what we hear can also reduce stress.

There are seven psychic ears, five more in addition to the right and left ears. If you are interested in exploring them, see the author's book, *Energy-Focused Meditation*.

Seeing

Seeing may be the most strongly developed sense for most of us. However, seeing can be very tricky in that one's perceptual abilities can focus on and remember some things and not others. It is rather like "tuning out" in our hearing ability. Therefore one can't always trust what one sees, unless a greater awareness is used. The greater awareness overrides the tuning out.

Sometimes we use the phrase "I see" to mean we comprehend what someone has shared with us, similar to the "I hear you" phrase. Some people have photographic memory. This allows them to go back to anything they have seen and totally recall it. It does have some wonderful applications; it's a great ability if you've left your grocery list at home.

Training yourself to see with greater awareness can be done by just focusing on what you see, looking away, and trying to recall things. Then look back and see what you missed. Repeating this several times can be quite helpful.

There are seven psychic eyes, five in addition to the right and left physical eyes. The next chapter contains information on them.

Developing the Senses

Our different body levels react to our senses in their own unique ways. The more each level develops its relationships with the senses, the more value we receive. The following meditation is lengthy and you may choose to do it in segments. Some of the answers you receive may be very enlightening, and make the time spent on the experience well worth the effort.

Meditation 2: Senses and the Physical Body

Begin by being in a meditative state.

1. Put your awareness in your physical body by focusing on your arms and legs.

2. Ask your physical body:

    a. What is its favorite smell? Least favorite smell?

    b. What does it most like to taste? Least favorite taste?

    c. What does it most like to touch? Least like to touch?

    d. What does it most like to hear? Least like to hear?

    e. What does it most like to see? Least like to see?

3. Ask your physical body: When is it most likely to open to instinct?

4. Ask your physical body: When is it most likely to open to knowing?

Meditation 3: Emotional (Astral) Body

1. Put your awareness in your emotional body by being aware of your navel and belly area.

2. You may then repeat questions 2 through 4 listed above.

Meditation 4: Mental Body

1. Put your awareness in your mental body by focusing on your forehead and brain area.

2. You may then repeat questions 2 through 4 listed in Meditation 2 above.

Meditation 5: Intuitional/
Compassionate Body

1. Put your awareness in your intuitional/compassionate body by focusing on the center of your chest and being aware of your heart energy.

2. You may then repeat questions 2 through 4 listed in Meditation 2.

Meditation 6: Will/
Spirit Body

1. Put your awareness in your will/spirit body by focusing on your back and the back of your heels.

2. You may then repeat questions 2 through 4 listed in Mediation 2.

Meditation 7: Soul Level Body

1. Put your awareness in your soul level body by focusing on the center of your forehead just below the hairline and all around the outside of the body.

2. You may then repeat questions 2 through 4 listed in Meditation 2.

Meditation 8: Divine Level Body

1. Put your awareness in your divine level body by focusing on the top of your head.

2. You may then repeat questions 2 through 4 listed in Meditation 2.

These meditations are also useful in that they help develop your use of the senses. By just focusing on the sense and the body, it helps open these areas. The more one focuses on an area, the greater the development.

Senses are such an important part of our lives. In addition to the warnings and information they give, we are blessed by the joyful and pleasurable aspects of the senses. In addition, all of the senses will lift us to higher consciousness levels if we fully open to them when in meditative states. To be fully alive certainly includes the use of the senses as well.

Chapter 6

The
Seven
Eyes

IN ADDITION TO the two physi-
cal eyes we humans use to see, five additional eyes are part
of our system. They make up our expanded awareness or
consciousness. They open spontaneously in our travels on
the evolutionary path. Occasionally one or more will open
prematurely—that is, before a person is able to handle or
understand the information or pictures that can appear.

Beginning with the third eye (located between the eyebrows) the five eyes are located on a line going straight
up the forehead. The fourth eye is just above the third
eye, the fifth is in the center of the forehead, the sixth is
just below the hairline, and the seventh about one inch
above the hairline. Each of the eyes has its own particular function and all are needed in a person's complete
development (see Figure 6.1, next page).

81

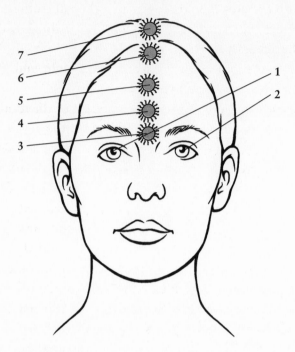

Figure 6.1 Location of the Seven Eyes

Our first two eyes have functions beyond our ordinary seeing abilities. The first eye, the right one, is primarily used in seeing the *forms* of objects. Along with seeing forms, distance, and detail, it also deals with other functions as well, which will be listed in the next chapter.

The second eye, the left one, relates more to our emotions. It gives us greater depth and a sense of relationship between objects viewed. It relates more to color and texture, rather than form.

Our third eye gives us understanding of the form and the working of our physical world. It enlarges on what the first eye sees.

Our fourth eye is for the understanding of relationships and development of belief in God. It enlarges on what is seen by the second eye.

Our fifth eye aids in understanding universal truths and ideals. With this eye we can receive concepts of the things we view, as well as the actual forms and workings.

Our sixth eye is necessary for true inner sight and the understanding of the essence and purpose of our lives.

Our seventh eye aids in the understanding of the totality of the universe and its purpose. Through sight of the seventh eye we receive divine understanding of events. The above descriptions are very brief and more information will be given in the next chapter.

Few of us have completely developed all seven eyes. In fact, very few have even the first two eyes fully developed. Much of it is due to unawareness of the possibilities in the various forms of sight. With proper development much can be added to our abilities in these areas. Much is due to our laziness in comprehending or seeing what our eyes actually view. Another reason for the poor development is not taking seriously our spiritual heritage of an expanded consciousness. All of these form "veils" over our eyes. As we remove the veils from our vision, new worlds open.

Dangers in Premature Opening

The main danger in premature opening of the eyes is in the inability to comprehend what we see, and the resultant fear it brings. Occasionally a person will have an eye "blown open" through use of drugs, a blow on the head, or other physical impact or through uneven development of their evolutionary process. Whatever the reason, if an eye is opened without fully understanding its purpose, the person can be confused and misunderstand the visions received. What should be a blessing sometimes feels like a curse.

If the third or fifth eyes are open, you may see geometric figures, lights, and colors. This may interfere with work or rest, or just be a nuisance. If this does happen, time should be given for the energy to flow through unhampered before starting work or attempting to rest. Fourth and sixth eyes will usually bring pictures of past, present, or future happenings in a symbolic or literal fashion. Rather than try to block the things we see, it is easier on the system if we let them flow through unhampered and really look at what is appearing. Hopefully, the following pages will open new worlds for your vision.

The Seven Eyes and Their Functions

Although each of the seven eyes has a separate and distinct function, they also work in combinations, and in full development all seven function together. All seven functioning together gives us the single eye. The more each eye is developed and the more they function together, the clearer our visions and the deeper our understandings of what we see in the world and beyond into the cosmos.

As our eyes are developed and function together, we may see into all areas, into oneself (the most difficult place to look), into others, into patterns of society, our planet, and into the cosmos, to understand the universal laws at work in all areas of life.

Our first, third, and fifth eyes have related functions, the higher the eye, the more detailed and intricate are the scenes we behold. The second and fourth eyes are also related and designed more to aid our understanding of life's processes. The sixth and seventh eyes aid us in the highest of spiritual understanding and sight.

First Eye

Our first eye is the right physical eye. This eye is used mainly for focusing on form, details, and distance. If you use this eye primarily, it means you are more interested in the structure of what you are viewing. This could also indicate being more interested in the structure of a relationship, and you are probably a more structured person by nature than someone who primarily uses the left eye.

When looking out of this eye, you usually have a tendency to be reserved or maintain your emotional composure. This is the eye for maintaining "dignity" and distance from others. It also helps focus control and awareness on the physical body.

As this eye is developed, you will begin to see many things you were totally unaware of previously. It is possible to see energy rain much as we see water raining on us. Energy pours onto the Earth all the time from the Sun, Moon, other planets, and other sources in the galaxy. By combining the forces of the first, third, and fifth eyes, you will be able to ascertain the differences in the energies. It is also possible to see other forms not normally seen with the naked eye.

Second Eye

The second eye is our left physical eye, and is used for ascertaining color, texture, and the relationship to what is viewed. You can readily see the necessity for an artist to have both of these eyes functioning well. Using this eye primarily, you will be willing to "see" with your emotions, and *feel* life rather than observe it as a first-eye person would. Using the second eye increases awareness of other people's expressions and feelings. It is also the eye we use when looking at people we love or trust.

Fear may cause this eye to cloud over or unfocus when looking at an object, person, or situation we fear. If we are unsure of ourselves or insecure, this clouding or unfocusing may also occur. When it does, we look from the right eye, and this brings more control and distance into our viewing.

When this eye begins to develop further, it is possible to see auras, astral entities, and scenes on the astral levels. At first, these things will appear very dimly, but as the second eye develops and veils are removed, they become increasingly clearer. When the first and second eyes are used together, we have two-dimensional sight.

Third Eye

The third eye is located between the eyebrows, and relates to our more mental functions. As mentioned, we see more deeply into physical things with this eye and have a much greater understanding of the nature of our world. Our physical world is made up of seven different forms of matter: solids, liquids, gases, and four types of ether. The physical eye readily sees solids, liquids, and some gases. All gases and ethers become visible in proportion to the development of the third eye. With a functioning third eye a person is able to see thought forms. Thoughts are energy and have form and color.

The clarity of the thought determines the color's vividness and the form's distinctness. The subject of the thought form determines the color. The strength of the thought form determines its longevity, and the distance the thought form can travel. Thought forms, ours and others, are in the air around us at all times. It is possible to know the content of the thought form by gently pushing them into our heads and being aware of what our thoughts turn to. An example of thought form power is when you have left to do something and can't remember what it was, and by returning to where you thought of it, you can usually remember it instantly. In that case, you moved faster than your thought form. Mental telepathy is a form of receiving thought forms and interpreting them. As this eye develops, it adds three-dimensional sight to our ordinary viewing. Most people have this developed to a certain extent but still have not fully reached the three-dimensional sight possible.

The second eye sees the astral (emotional) auras and with the third eye it is possible to see the auras of the mental body. Everything is brighter and colors are more vivid with the introduction of the third eye energy into the everyday physical eye viewing. In meditations, clouds of color often appear, as well as the simpler geometric forms and energy patterns mentioned previously.

Fourth Eye

This eye is related to our intuitional selves and the fourth plane or level of evolution. It is located just above the third eye. As this eye develops, we see with more understanding and increased awareness of the relationships: humans and humans, humans and nature, humans and the spiritual world. This is the eye of the fourth dimension, seeing into it, being aware of density and hollowness. If, on meeting someone, you have a feeling that they are hollow or solid, you may be seeing their energy patterns with your fourth eye.

In meditation, with the use of the fourth eye, one can see one's own patterns of behavior as well as others and be more aware of how actions and reactions operate and cause us to react in particular ways. The background color of the fourth eye is usually black and figures have a whitish outline and are much like shadows in front of bright windows or light. This helps us to see the patterns of action and interaction.

Fifth Eye

The fifth eye is related to the will/spirit part of ourselves and the fifth plane or level of evolution. It is located in the center of the forehead and is sometimes called the third eye, too. The background, as seen in meditations, is sometimes a combination of dark red, purple, and dark blue colors. It may be said to have some of the colors of outer space. In the early stages of development these colors are muddy, but as development increases, the colors become clear, intense, and bright. This may then be truly called the "outer space vision center."

When the developed vision of this eye is combined with the physical eyes (one and two), then x-ray vision may occur. X-ray vision is to see into an object much as an x-ray machine does. This has a somewhat two-dimensional effect at first, but as the sight becomes more developed, one can see in three-dimensional vision.

It is possible with this eye to see around objects, as well as into them. Here one becomes able to bend the energy from the eye. It aids in being aware of the parts of an object in relationship to the whole. One can learn to see through buildings, mountains, or other objects as well as around them.

As well as seeing more intricate geometric forms and patterns, this eye is also used for seeing into the nature of the universe. It is possible to receive concepts of the universe's workings. What you may see in a split second may take you many minutes or even hours to fully explain or comprehend.

When this eye has some development and is combined with the first and second eyes, physical objects seem to light up and have their own luminous glow. Looking *at* colors becomes looking *into* colors. A colored paper, for instance, becomes three-dimensional in sight.

This is an excellent area in which to explore time and space, for looking into trees, plants, animals, and people in order to observe their energy patterns and movements. It is also an excellent level for observing the akashic records. (The akashic records are the records of our lives past, present, and probable futures.) It is possible to view these records from lower eyes, but many times it is in symbolic form or partially symbolic in form which may cause some confusion. Viewing from this level gives clarity and also shows karmic interaction and interconnecting links between people and events. This is also the eye center for "getting it together." If you have trouble with spacing out or not being in control of your thoughts, concentrating on this eye will help bring you together.

Sixth Eye

The sixth eye is related to our soul level and to the sixth plane, or level, of evolution. It is the level for seeing into the essence of things and their places in the system of evolution. It is located just below the hairline. With development of this eye you can see the soul radiance of others and can be aware of their soul "sound" or soul "vibratory" pattern. In combination with the other eyes, it allows you to see another person's purpose in life, to understand them and their behavior on the deepest levels. With this functioning, one can begin to form universal level friendships which are above time, space, and personalities—the ultimate in friendships.

The activities of the sixth eye include seeing into the sixth dimension, which includes not only the sight of the fifth dimension, but also the very fine energy lines that tie one thing to another, one event to another. It is also the level where you see the radiance of all things, not just the luminous glow of the fifth-eye sight, but the inner radiance and divine energy inherent in all matter.

Seventh Eye

The seventh eye is located about three-quarters of an inch to one inch above the hairline, and is a part of the chakra system that rings the crown chakra. (Chakras are energy vortices in our systems.) It is related to the divine in our nature and to the seventh plane, or level, of evolution. From this eye one can see a panoramic view of life. One can also see into the highest ether. The view sometimes resembles a curved mirror and the picture will be in reverse as it is reflected.

The first sight most people get from this eye is a dull white glow, which increases in clarity and radiance as the eye is developed. This can extend to cover the entire forehead and later the entire system. When fully developed it is possible to see the blinding radiance, the divine radiance, as St. Paul did. Seeing life from this eye will help you understand the oneness of all, the underlying connections of all in the cosmos, the heavens, and beyond the heavens. Even beginning sight helps in the understanding of all life. It is also possible to see spiritual personages through this level. Although they may be seen through the lower eyes, viewing through this level brings a oneness and understanding.

This is the level of the seventh dimension, the most complicated of all, and the most clear. This is the level of paradoxes becoming one, the deepest unity possible. All the complexity, the intricacy of the divine plan, becomes crystal clear and amazingly simple on this level. It is also possible to see the seven-dimensional scene coalesce into one dimension, the ultimate in oneness.

When we are in the fourth through the seventh eyes, we are in spiritual levels and are above time and space. All time, past, present, and future, are now. All places are here.

Development of Vision

There are three main areas first needed for developing the seven eyes and the ability to function through these eyes. First, removing the veils or blocks which hinder our sight; second, learning to focus the energies; third, being open and aware in order to receive and interpret a vision. ("Vision" used in this chapter refers to something seen by *other* than the physical eyes. It may or may not have spiritual implications.) Another way of explaining the three areas is:

1. Clearing a path;

2. Focusing energy; and

3. Opening to functional use of the energy.

The first step, removing the veils and blocks, for many may be the most difficult. A healthful diet, with many "live" (that is *uncooked*) foods such as salads, fruits, nuts, and vegetables will aid in refining and purifying our bodies and energies. Proper breathing and exercise are necessary also. Cleansing the system is a part of removing these veils and blocks. This includes removing prejudices, rigid attitudes, emotional blocks as well as a proper elimination for the entire physical body. All that is not needed for a healthy system should be properly eliminated, be it food, drink, emotions, or thoughts. In the beginning it is more difficult to build up the body and cleanse the system, but as one progresses it becomes a part of one's nature to care for oneself.

The second step, learning to focus the energies, is a matter of using one's mind power over the energies. Practicing meditation exercises, becoming aware of your energies, and moving them from place to place are good ways to begin to get the control you need.

The third step, being open, aware, and actively receptive, is for many people quite difficult as it means letting go of thoughts. It means letting pictures, words, or feelings enter the system without being censored, blocked, or ignored. Many times we will look at a part of a picture or vision and quickly make our own judgment about its message. The better way is to observe the entire picture or vision and let it speak its message to you. Sometimes the meaning can be very foreign to our present beliefs and attitudes, and we do need to be open to these other possibilities.

Usually we have one eye that is more developed than another. It is also possible to have the higher eyes open for a moment, so quickly that one is not aware of the area from which the picture came. At times it happens so quickly we are almost unaware that anything did happen, and we pay little or no attention to it. At a later time, a fleeting memory of it may return. Each picture, each symbol, has a message for us, and being aware of them and their meanings will aid us in our growth and enjoyment of that growth and life in general.

As our eyes become more developed, the pictures we see become much larger. They may be larger than your head, both in length and breadth. Sometimes the pictures may appear inside your head and sometimes they are visible in front of your head. This is an indication you are beginning to project the images naturally, and is also a sign that your visual powers are increasing. It is possible to project the pictures onto a wall or screen and then watch the action. If others are developed enough with their vision, they may watch your pictures as you do.

Eyes one, three, and five are controlled mainly by the pituitary gland. Eyes two and four are controlled by the pineal gland. Both the pituitary and pineal glands affect the sixth and seventh levels. In higher work, the hypothalamus may have the main effect on these eyes.

Techniques for Meditations

To begin, first find a quiet area where you can be undisturbed, relaxed, and open. As you continue to practice, you will find you can do the exercises most anyplace. It is best, also, not to be too hungry, or to do the exercises just after eating.

In order to keep a flow, you may wish to record these exercises on a tape. Otherwise you may wish to have a friend read them, or even lead you in the exercises. It is possible to read them as you do them, but it would be best to read over each one completely first.

What to Expect from the Meditations

Most people will see or feel something the first time they do the exercise. If you don't, you may be trying too hard. You have to *let it happen.* The following are ways some people experience psychic pictures:

Literal: The picture may be how an event happened, or a most probable future event. If you received a probable future event, ask if there are alternatives if you don't like what you have seen. If you like the alternative better, ask for that. You may even ask what strengthens the possible futures and what weakens them.

Symbolic: This is the way most people see events or patterns. If you receive information in what you believe to be symbolic form, ask the symbol what it means or what it has to say to you. Then be open and listen. Many times a much deeper meaning comes through a symbolic picture.

Anything we see is always correct—either an actual or a probable event. However, interpreting what it relates to and how it relates can be 100 percent wrong. Be careful not to jump to conclusions about the meanings. Try to keep your emotions and thoughts out of it, so the interpretation is clearer.

Symbols are formed by the answer or impression going through your subconscious energy pattern. The answer or impression is then absorbed into the symbol that it most closely resembles. Thus the energy of the answer is turned into the energy of your symbol that may be more meaningful to you.

Many people hear answers in words. But be careful it is not your own thoughts. If you are truly open and detached, it is probably not your thoughts. Careful attention will help you to discern which are your thoughts, other's thoughts, or spiritual insights. Some people get a feeling of "knowing" rather than seeing or hearing. They do not know how or why they know; they just know that they know. It is a deep, inner conviction.

Occasionally we may both see and hear, or may see, hear, and know all at the same time. Obviously this is the best way, and is an indication of many levels being open at once. This method usually brings its own interpretation and clarification.

Meditation 1: Warm Ups

1. **Breathing Exercises:** Sitting or lying down, close your eyes. Begin to breathe deeply and slowly, bringing the air down into your body and exhale through your feet. This helps to ground you. Grounding gives you balance, strength, and freedom to soar in your meditations.

   a. Then begin to bring the breath up into your head and out your forehead. This clears the forehead.

   b. After doing both of the above for a few minutes, do both at the same time for a minute.

   c. Breathe normally.

2. **Relaxing into Strength:** Relax into strength, don't relax into weakness. Let loose and feel your energy. Weakness is not relaxation, it's giving up—dying a little. Feel strength, relaxed strength, life flowing through you. Relax into alertness and awareness. Still your mind and body so you can be truly alert and aware. Let your relaxations and meditations be a springboard into life.

3. **Twilight Zone:** This is an excellent exercise for training oneself to get into different states of consciousness without falling asleep, losing consciousness, or going into a trance. Also it is excellent for helping you to maintain full consciousness while you sleep, to help you remember your dreams, to be more alert in everyday life, and to learn to control your mind and keep it still.

   a. Let your body, mind, and emotions be still. Try to get into the twilight zone between sleep and wakefulness. Be totally relaxed and alert. Don't look for anything, but if you hear anything or see anything be aware of it but let it pass on its way. Be aware but don't hang on.

   b. You may find your breathing is more in the front of your chest and more peaceful and easy. As you continue, your breathing begins to encompass your entire chest and diaphragm area. The deeper you get into the twilight zone, the deeper but lighter your breathing. Your mind may begin to feel as though it can see and hear in all directions. Five minutes is long enough to hold this state in the beginning. Later you may wish to increase the time as it becomes comfortable for you.

   c. Stretch completely.

4. **Stretching:** Always end a meditation with a thorough stretch. It helps put you together and helps you to go deeper with the next exercise.

Meditation Exercises

The following is a group of meditation exercises that will help develop and strengthen the psychic eyes.

Meditation 2: Open Meditation

Starting with the first eye and continuing with each eye in turn, let the energy flow out and flow in at the same time. The energy flows should be circular. The energy may flow out in a clockwise or counterclockwise manner. This happens at the outer edge of the eyes or chakras. The inflow of energy then flows in closer to the center.

Don't look for anything in particular, just be aware if you do see something. Put your main awareness on the energy process.

Meditation 3: Viewing and Moving the White Dot

You may lie down, or sit cross-legged, or in a lotus position. Make sure you are comfortable and sitting erect. Massage your forehead and top of your head. Breathe peacefully and deeply.

Focus your attention on the third eye, letting energy flow in and out. Concentrate on this area. Then let the concentration go and be open and aware. Visualize a white dot of light. Breathe into it until it becomes clear.

Then slowly move the dot of light up to the fourth eye, breathe into it, then repeat with the fifth, sixth, and the seventh eye. As the dot moves up it should expand and become more brilliant.

After the seventh eye, move it to the crown chakra on the top of the head. Let the white dot be filled with radiance, breathe into it, and let it expand until it seems to fill your entire head.

Then slowly bring the white light back down to the seventh eye, sixth, fifth, fourth, and then the third eye, trying to keep the radiance and the expansion.

Breathe into it and let your mind be rejuvenated by spiritual energy.

This exercise expands the spiritual influence in all areas of vision.

Meditation 4: Alternate Route

Begin as in the previous exercise.

After the white dot of light becomes clear in the third eye, bring it back to the spine, and then up to and out of the crown chakra. Let it expand and become radiant there. Let it be filled with spiritual energy, and then bring it back to the third eye the same way you lead it up.

Hold it in the third eye while you meditate without focusing on anything. Just be expanded and open.

Meditation 5: Vitality Globules

This is an exercise to practice outdoors on a sunny day. Vitality globules are minute, clear dots of pure energy in the air. They contain prana from the sun, and the more sunlight present, the more globules and the faster they dance in the air. Although they are clear, shadings of color may be seen in them.

Practice this exercise outdoors on a sunny day.

With your first three eyes open and energized, observe the air. Concentrate more energy in the first eye. Watch the air near you. The vitality globules are continually moving about—it is almost impossible to concentrate or look at one for long. It's like trying to follow the movement of a snowflake, only they are smaller and faster.

Meditation 6: Energy Movement

Practice this exercise outdoors.

1. Have your first three eyes open, with emphasis on energy in the third eye. Observe a tree or plant. As

you continue to do this, you should begin to see energy moving in the tree or plant.

2. The same may be done with other people. Be sure you give them the same respect you would expect for yourself, and don't pry.

Meditation 7: Fourth-Eye Emphasis

1. Have your first four eyes open with emphasis on energy in the fourth eye. Look into a candle flame. What is it like inside?

2. In the dark, look into objects and see their light—not the outer glow, but the inner light. It is possible to determine objects by their lights.

3. Observe your friends and be aware of yourself at the same time. What are your energy patterns in your interactions as you observe from this level?

Meditation 8: Fifth-Eye Emphasis

1. With your first five eyes open and emphasis on the fifth eye, allow the energy from the fifth eye to curve around objects and see behind them.

2. Doing the above step, look into objects, see the depth inside.

3. Again, doing the above steps, look through objects and see what is behind them.

   With the same energy pattern, meditate on colors, allowing different shadings and tones to appear. Be aware of shades that are different from what we know physically now.

   With the same energy pattern, ask for a concept of time or of space. Be open and allow the picture to form. Allow the picture to fill your body so that you get a deeper understanding of it and can retain it longer.

Meditation 9: Sixth-Eye Emphasis

1. **Outdoors:** Have the first six eyes open with emphasis on the sixth. Be aware that you are living in a part of the universe, a very small part. Then be aware of the life that goes on in this part of which you normally are not aware.

2. **Traveling:** Be aware of our planet in relationship to the universe. Be aware of transversing a planet. Do not do this while operating the vehicle yourself. It may take your concentration away from where it is needed.

3. **Spiritual Beings:** It is possible to see the energy forms of spiritual beings with the sixth eye. They appear in the sky and sometimes close to the earth.

Meditation 10: Seventh-Eye Emphasis

1. **Outdoors:** Have all seven eyes open, with emphasis on the seventh. Be aware of nature and yourself. Be aware of the ties between yourself and nature, the oneness. Be aware of insects, birds, and animals, and observe them and their actions in relationship to the total universe. Their existence is as important in the divine scheme of life as is ours.

2. **Prayer:** When praying, have energy in all seven eyes with emphasis on the seventh. Praying in this manner may cause you to change your prayers while praying, as you receive new depth of understanding on this level. You may also see pictures of how your prayers will be answered or why you

should not request a particular thing. This is enlightened prayer.

Meditation 11: Full Consciousness— Past and Present

Massage your eyes and the back of your neck. Breathe deeply and peacefully.

With your eyes open, concentrate on looking out of the first eye. Be aware of form and detail.

Concentrate on looking out of your left eye. Be aware of colors and relationships of objects in view.

Close your first and second eyes, equalize the energy in both and move the energy up to the third eye. Let the third eye be open, expanded, and aware.

Move the energy up to each of the other eyes, letting them be open, expanded, and aware.

Keeping some energy in the seventh eye, let energy flow back to the other eyes and let yourself *be in full consciousness*. Be aware of other times in your life when you felt this same consciousness. Bring this memory deep into your awareness. (Do not hold this state for more than five minutes in the beginning, as it releases much energy.) You may wish to make notes of what you remember and review it as a way to help retain the full consciousness for longer periods of time. By full consciousness in this exercise, we mean full consciousness you are capable of at the present. Most people use only a small part of their consciousness in their daily lives.

Meditation 12: Seeing a Picture

Look at a picture with the first two eyes. Do this from a comfortable distance. With energy in the right eye, observe the picture. Pay special attention to form and detail.

With energy in the left eye, observe the picture. Pay special attention to color, mood, and balance of objects in the picture.

With energy equalized in both these eyes, observe the picture. Compare the difference from the first time you looked at the picture.

Look at the picture with each of the other eyes in turn, then with all seven. How does it look different to you now as compared to the first time you looked at it?

Meditation 13: Knowing Yourself

Be in a calm, peaceful state with right and left eyes open. Let energy flow out of the right eye. Observe the scene in front of you. Let yourself expand and be joyful. How much expansion and joy are you comfortable with?

Let energy flow out of the left eye. Again observe the scene in front of you. Think of significant relationships in your life. How much energy do you feel free to exchange with others? Would you rather receive? Or would you rather give?

Close these eyes and let the third eye be open. With this vision look into your body. What do you find? Is it a healthy, functioning body? You may wish to visualize correcting any problems.

Open the fourth eye. Visualize yourself in relationship to others. Watch your actions, be aware of your moods and the way you talk. Does it seem comfortable to have you around? How do you come across?

Open the fifth eye. Ask to be shown a past life that has an effect on this life. If you do not understand what you see, ask for clarification.

Open the sixth eye. Ask for information regarding a purpose you have in this life. Are you working for or against it?

Open the seventh eye. Ask to be shown an effect you have on our planet. Then ask to be shown the effect others have on you.

Meditation 14: Dimensions of a Relationship

Do this exercise with a friend. Sit facing each other.

With energy in your right eye, observe your physical body. Where do you feel tight? Open? What would your physical body like to do with this person?

With energy in your left eye, observe your emotions, feelings. How does this person affect you emotionally? How do you affect the person emotionally?

Equalize the energy in the right and left eyes. Then move the energy emphasis to the third eye. Be aware of the third dimension of your relationship. How does your relationship affect others close to you, others close to your friend? How can you improve situations?

Bring energy up to the fourth eye and continue to gaze at your friend. How does this relationship affect your life goals, your lifestyle? Is it helpful or unhelpful in your relations with others in your career and community? How can you improve situations?

Bring energy up to the fifth eye, continue the gaze. Be aware of your karmic patterns in the friendship. What are you trying to fulfill in this relationship? To work out? To balance between you? To understand? Close your right and left eyes and ask for a picture of a past life that affects the relationship at this time. How does the working out of your karma affect the balance of energy on our planet?

Bring energy up to the sixth eye and again gaze at your friend. Be aware of the force of the energy in your relationship. Be aware of how each of you has always existed and always will exist. Be aware of how sometimes you are in relationship and sometimes you are not. Whether or not you are in a relationship, there are still universal ties. Are the universal ties between you strong?

Bring energy up to the seventh eye. Be aware of the oneness of the two of you. Your problems and joys are each other's. As one of you grows, so does the other. Be aware of how no one is alone. We are all parts of one another.

Meditation 15: Telepathy

With a friend, take turns sending pictures to each other and trying to receive them. Use the third and fifth eyes separately and together.

Meditation 16: Sounds

Let each eye in turn be energized. As each is energized, listen for sounds inside your head. These may include ringing bells, waterfalls, wind, oceans, or the sounds of music. Opening the visual areas also affects our auditory areas.

Visualization Powers

There are two forms of visualization. One is the practice of picturing in your mind something you want either in your life or for someone else. This sends out a force into the universe to bring the particular item, quality, opportunity, or right people to you or another person.

The second form of visualization is to ask for a picture of what is already in your probable future for you or whatever you have a question about.

Obviously it seems wisest to ask what is the most probable future and then use the first form of visualization to ensure its happening, or to use the first form to change the probable future, if you do not appreciate what you saw in the first visualization.

Visualization is one of our strongest tools to shape our presents and our futures. It should be used wisely. Be sure you want what you visualize—you might get it. Visualization is a form of prayer which adds mental energy to the already powerful prayer energy. Powers of visualization are increased many times if you can feel the visualization in your entire body and feel that you already have what you are picturing. In order not to limit yourself to what your own mind can conceive, ask for what you want, or something better. Keep in mind that God's will should come before yours.

Meditation 17: Future

If you are doubtful about your future, with the help of your fifth eye energy, you may ask and see what your probable futures are in a given area. (Some areas are blocked from our visioning for our own protection.) Ask for a picture of what you can do in order to strengthen the force of the probable future you most wish for, or feel is best for you. Then visualize this happening and feel it in your entire system.

Meditation 18: Health

If you are in ill health or have a health problem, do not visualize the illness or problem. This only increases it. Instead visualize yourself in perfect health, and feel the visualization in your entire body.

Meditation 19: Prosperity

If you would like more prosperity, visualize yourself being prosperous and enjoying it and using it wisely.

Feel this in your entire body. However, visualizing a particular way of becoming prosperous may block other opportunities.

Meditation 20: Visualizing for Others

Do not visualize things for other people unless they have asked for your assistance. Otherwise you are meddling in their lives. However, visualizing spiritual qualities for anyone can be a blessing for them, and for you. Remember the energy we send out for others comes back for us, too.

Meditation 21: Morning Awareness

In the morning, ask for a picture of what your day is likely to bring to you. If there are things you do not like, ask for an understanding of them. Then use your visualization powers to change things or to make your day more loving and beautiful. Some people may *feel* what the day will be like, rather than *see* it.

Meditation 22: Abundance

God has far more beautiful things and more abundance for us than we can imagine. Our problem is we are so closed that we do not take them. In fact, most of the time we do not even know the gifts are there.

In the morning, breathe peacefully and deeply, and open the entire chest area. Take in the breath of life that is yours. Ask God to help you be open to receive the abundance God has for you. Feel it in your entire system. Keep the openness to receiving with you.

Meditation 23: Relationships

Visualize being more loving, understanding, and open to the joys and sorrows of being a true friend. (Sorrow has a positive side—it can stretch us and help us to understand and appreciate life.)

Meditation 24: Self

Don't forget yourself! Visualize whatever you feel you need most. Feel it in your entire body. It can be inner strength, ability to do these exercises better, spiritual qualities, or just for an openness to really be completely yourself.

Every time we do a visualization, we plant a seed. Some seeds take longer to germinate than others. Some plants take a much longer time for maturity than others. So you will find that some of the visualizations are answered immediately, and others may take years. Prayer is the strongest form of energy available to us. Visualization added to our prayer energy makes it even more powerful. Enjoy it, but use it wisely. If in doubt, go to the top— ask for God's guidance in your prayer visualizations.

When first practicing these exercises, you may sense openness and relaxation in your forehead or entire head. If they are over-done, it may result in headaches, nervousness, or a release of emotional and mental blocks at a rate faster than you care to handle them. I caution you not to overdo the exercises. A slower, steady pace will help you develop faster than overdoing and then having to quit for a while. I also realize that some will choose to overdo any-way. Physical exercise and sleep are two excellent ways to recover.

You may find it rewarding to keep a journal of your experiences and insights. Many times you see things which aren't completely understood at the time, and it can be very helpful to review the journal as your growth increases.

This chapter gives only a very small portion of the information and experiences available with the development of the seven eyes. Whole areas have not been touched on. Many of you will discover these other areas for yourselves. This chapter is designed to give you some methods for opening these areas and to make you aware of the possibilities awaiting you in the total life.

Chapter 7

Consciousness

THE DEVELOPMENT OF our consciousness, or awareness, is one of the most important parts of our growth. If we are not aware of, or conscious of, something, that has happened or is happening, then we don't know what may be affecting us. Therefore, we not only don't receive learning from the situation, we also aren't able to make choices. We are just left with intangibles, which may cause us to react in ways we wouldn't if we had been more aware.

The same is true in spiritual growth. Actually most people are more highly developed then they realize. Their awareness may not be developed to the point they recognize all they know about other areas and learning. When they do open to new concepts, sometimes its as though they have always known these things, and they may have. They just didn't know what they knew. Therefore one of the first steps in growth is to develop consciousness so they can make usable all they already know in daily life.

There are many ways to increase your recognition of knowledge. Anything that can trigger your memory is helpful, such as reading or listening to speakers. Practicing meditations to develop consciousness can be very helpful. Increasing one's brain power is very important, since it is through the brains that we process a great deal of this information. Our bodies process some, however it is still through the brains that the major work of consciousness is done. The following are some meditations to help increase your consciousness:

Meditation 1: Watching Your Feelings

Each day take some time to just sit with your feelings and thoughts. Observe how much you can be aware of them. Check out different parts of your body. Do they feel different from other parts? Sometimes there will be things you wish to do about these feelings, and that can be very helpful. Being in tune with your body and being conscious of what is happening there can help you make better choices for your system.

Meditation 2: Watching Your Thoughts

Each day take time to sit with your thoughts and let them think themselves. Just let your mind ramble. If it sticks on negative things, note them and then raise your consciousness through deep breathing or listening to music or by going for a walk. It is not helpful to get stuck in negativity and just dwell in it. Get some information from it and then move on to higher levels. Some people are quite surprised at how much of their thinking process consists of dwelling on things in a negative way. Looking for the positive side of situations can also help.

Meditation 3: Recurring Memories

If a situation from the past keeps coming back to you, go into it and ask yourself what you haven't yet learned from it. There may also be actions that need to be taken because of it.

Higher Consciousness

Our spiritual makeup calls for our opening up to higher levels of consciousness; our evolution pushes in that direction. Focusing only on the human level of consciousness is not enough for most people, and expansion into the higher levels of consciousness has exploded in the last few decades. From indications of peoples' directions and astrological configurations, it looks like the explosion of growth will continue.

Although some of this evolution into higher levels is happening almost automatically, with many people opening their belief systems, it still takes time and dedication to open to these higher levels in significant ways. However, working with this process is worth it, as increased creativity and productivity can come from it, as well as the ability to be more loving and compassionate.

Life doesn't necessarily become less complex as we grow, actually in some cases the increased energy available to the person complicates life even more. However, with the new skills and understanding of life coming from higher consciousness levels, most people find wonderful new skills for better living. There are several ways that can help you develop higher consciousness:

1. Spend more time in meditation and prayer.

2. Read and study about higher levels.

3. Developing intuitive skills will help in living with the higher energies.

Reality of Consciousness Levels

All levels of consciousness have their own reality, however, there may be no permanence beyond the moment the consciousness is perceived, because we would view the same things differently at another time. Truth and reality have many faces.

Reality is such a strange thing. When we are in a dream state, that seems real to us. When in heavy emotional states, that is a powerful reality, but it, too, can evaporate when understood from higher levels. When we are on high, spiritual, transcendent levels, our human existence fades in a greater reality. Whatever level you are at or focus on, you will find a reality that is from that area. Wherever you focus, *there* is your reality. People who do not recognize this can spend a good deal of time being upset or ineffective, because they fail to deal with the reality they are facing, or to recognize they can change realities.

Our everyday human existence has a great deal of reality to us. However, as we reach higher levels, we can look at human existence as having no permanence and no reality. However, while we are in this human existence, it is real and we need to deal with it on its level. If we try to attach too much to the belief system that human life is not real, but a dream, we may miss the lessons and growth for which we are spending time as humans. This, in turn, could hold us back from the larger or next step in existence. Recognizing that our human life is not our main existence gives a better perspective on life in general. As we develop our consciousness levels, it becomes apparent that we have a great deal of choice in forming and reforming our own realities.

Developing the Brains

There are many ways of increasing the brain's power. Someone has said we only use about ten percent of our brains. If that test were repeated in the 1990s, it is possible a much higher score would be achieved. Certainly intelligence has increased for many persons. Our schools sometimes are not able to keep up with the need to develop brain skills, however, many people are doing their own developing. The following meditations are some ways to increase the development of the brains.

Meditation 4: Walking

Many people like to walk and think. They feel it clears their heads and opens them to new ideas. How you walk can also open particular areas of your brains. Below are some forms of walking, which you might find energizes and stimulate your brain areas. (For locations of the brain areas, refer to Figures 7.1 and 7.2, page 112.)

1. **Right Brain:** As you walk, swing your left arm and open your neck area. You should be able to feel the energy going up through your neck and head into your right brain. The reason for keeping the neck area open is that is where most people block energy going to the head. It sometimes causes headaches or neck aches.

2. **Left Brain:** Walk swinging your right arm and open your neck area. You should be able to feel energy going into your head and into your left brain.

   Note that sitting in a chair and doing the same exercises can also help.

3. **Left Brain, Right Brain,** and **Corpus Callosum** (bridge between the brains): Swinging both arms alternately, as you walk, energizes and activates these three areas. Keep the neck area open and feel the entire neo-mammalian system (left brain, right brain, and corpus callosum) opening.

4. **Limbic System:** When walking, accentuate swinging your hips. Again, be open in the neck area and feel the energies running into the midbrain system.

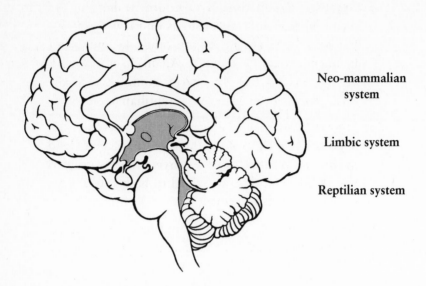

Figure 7.1 Physically Developed Brains

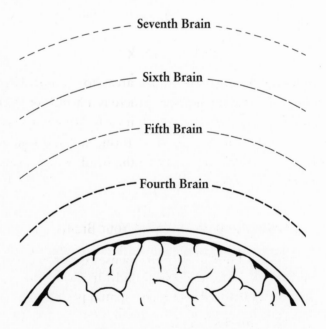

Figure 7.2 Etheric Brains

5. **Reptilian Brain:** Imagine you are walking on an area about as wide as a rail, as on railroad tracks. Put one foot in front of the other, keeping your balance as best as you can. Again, keep the neck area open and feel the energy going up into the lower back of the head to the reptilian area.

6. **Fourth Brain:** For this exercise, walk evenly and peacefully with open palms of the hands held against each other as if in prayer (fingers pointed up). Your head does not need to be bowed, but a prayerful attitude is helpful.

   Again, keep the neck open and feel energy going through your head to the area above it, where the fourth-brain energy is located.

7. **Fifth** through **Seventh Brains:** Walk the same way as indicated above, however each time feeling you are focusing above your head in the area of the particular brain area you are focusing on.

Brain Check

Periodically checking into your brain areas to see how they are doing can help activate them. Also if there is a health problem or a blocking problem it is easier to catch it early. We will work with the three brain levels in the physical form, and the four other brains still in the etheric stage above the head. Below are some meditations to help in this process.

Meditation 5: Checking Your Brains

1. **Reptilian Brain:** This brain focuses on protection and survival of the physical body. It also relates to space or territorial issues and spatial perceptions.

   a. Tune into this brain.

b. Do you feel comfortable there?

c. Are there stuck areas?

d. Ask how it is doing with its work.

e. Ask it to increase its consciousness. Breathe into it, which will focus the flow of prana to that area.

f. What information comes from the increased awareness?

g. Does the brain need something from you?

2. **Limbic System:** This brain area relates to our emotional body with all its feeling and motivational aspects. Follow steps listed above under reptilian brain.

3. **Neo-mammalian System:** This system contains the right and left brains and the corpus callosum. It relates to thinking, reasoning, creating, and other forms of mental activity. They work best together. In the meditation you may wish to do them together or separately, or perhaps both. Follow instructions listed above under reptilian brain.

Fourth through Seventh Brains

Scientists say the neo-mammalian system took two million years to develop. We don't know how long it will take for the fourth through seventh brains to be a part of our physical system, and they may never, remaining instead a part of our etheric or spiritual makeup. They can, however, function if a person focuses on them and "thinks" in their areas. Life is becoming so complex that we need to do more of this type of transcendent thinking. Many people may find they automatically use the higher brains when the need arises for creative, spiritual, or higher mental activities. Most people, when consciously working with these areas for the first time, are surprised by how much they already use them.

For these four levels the following meditation may be used:

Meditation 6: Checking Etheric Brains

Do the exercise for each of the brains, in turn.

1. Focus on the area above the head in the brain energy with which you wish to relate.

2. Energize the area by visualizing prana going into it.

3. Ask if it is awakened and usable.

4. Ask how much you use it.

5. Ask for what purposes it likes to be used.

6. Ask for some information from it at this time.

Meditation 7: Checking Brain Levels
Eight Through Twelve

Do the same exercise as for fourth through seventh. These levels continue above level seven.

Developing a Memory Bridge

Many of us, when first meditating to receive information, will be aware of messages or visions, but will not be able to remember them. We don't have the "bridge" developed between the higher and regular consciousness levels. Sometimes this is a problem because the three lower brains don't have the conceptual skills to readily process the information.

Another problem is that we sometimes start judging the vision or messages right away, and this pulls the energy out of the moment, and the information is gone. The following meditation can help develop some skills in developing the bridge so that memory can be retained.

Meditation 8: Building a Memory Bridge

Note: It is best if you read all of the directions first so that you don't break your concentration. You may want someone to guide you in this meditation.

1. Open and relax your brain areas. Breathe into your entire head and relax the area. Feel as though you are letting loose of the thinking processes.

2. Focus on one of the higher brains or focus on higher spiritual levels you readily reach through some of your regular meditations.

3. In order to facilitate the receiving of a message or a vision, ask a question in the area of the higher brain or higher spiritual level. Be open.

4. When you receive a message or see a vision, feel it in your body. While you hold the information in your body, review it, in order to strengthen the memory. The body is usually not as restricted as the brains. The body then acts as a transformer so the brains can comprehend and retain memories. By receiving the information in the body, it helps develop the greater conceptual skills in the brain.

5. Write the information down and review it again. Now is the time to ponder and judge any visions or messages, especially in terms of how you can make them work in your life.

The more you practice this, the easier it gets. One day you will notice that it is automatic. You will know your bridge from higher consciousness to human consciousness is completed.

Colors and Consciousness

Working with colors is a way of energizing the system and increasing consciousness of information or problems in your system. Colors are manifestations of the frequencies or vibrations of energy with which we deal every day. The more of these vibrations you can relate with well, the more expansive your consciousness is and the greater flexibility you have in life.

Some people actually see the colors, while others imagine the colors or sense the color in the body. If a color rushes into your body, you will know you had a lack of that particular vibration in your system. Sometimes you will feel that your body is drinking in the color. That, too, is an indication you may be short of that vibration. If one is difficult or uncomfortable, then there is something in the vibration of the color to which your body has some resistance, or you haven't developed it well. The following list of twelve colors can be of great help when imagined or visualized in the body for at least a few minutes each.

Meditation 9: Colors and Consciousness

Bring each color into your body, one at a time. Let your mind ramble and be aware of feelings or thoughts arising while the particular color is in your system. Some people like to stop and make notes when information comes to them.

1. Pink (some prefer fuschia pink)
2. Red
3. Coral
4. Orange
5. Gold
6. Yellow

7. Yellow/green

8. Green

9. Aqua

10. Blue

11. Lilac

12. Purple

The above colors represent the primary, secondary, and tertiary colors. Some people like to end the meditation with filling themselves with a vibrant light. A white light is acceptable, but a clear vibrant light has higher energies. The darker levels of these colors relate to inner levels, and can be used to open and activate these areas. If there are black or jagged streaks in any of the colors, it usually indicates that negativity is present in that vibration. If so, you may want to know what the negativity is so you can release it. Usually by asking the consciousness what the problem is, through the color, information will come. Otherwise you may wish to change the color to a very light, more spiritual version of the vibration. The more white, the more spiritual. However, if the color is pale or faded looking, it may not be well developed or lack strength. Muddy colors can also indicate little development or use.

A solid black usually means unknown or potential. Sometimes it is a velvety or shiny black. If you see this in your meditations, you may wish to flood it with vibrant light to release the message of the potential so you will know what is possible.

The Brain Stem

The area of the brain stem and just above it has some very powerful energies with expanded consciousness. Besides the top of the brain stem, the area includes the thalamus, pineal, and pituitary glands (see Figure 7.3, opposite page). Activated together they can expand consciousness.

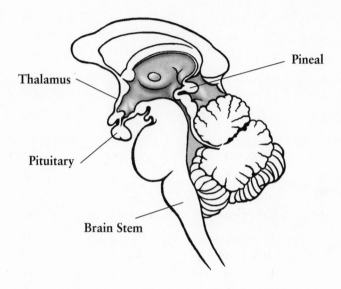

Figure 7.3 Brain Stem and Related Areas

The following are several meditations for that purpose. (I do not recommend doing very many bodies at a time—perhaps three or four—as one can get too far into altered states from this meditation and find it difficult to function well afterwards. Sometimes visualizing the color of watermelon red in one's head can help bring consciousness back to a normal state.)

Meditation 10: Expanding Body Consciousness

1. Focus on the top of the brain stem, the thalamus, pineal, and pituitary glands.

2. Imagine you are breathing into that area. This will help you increase the prana and energy in that area.

3. Be aware of your physical body by focusing on your arms and legs.

4. Send energy from the brain stem and above area into your physical body.

5. Open your awareness. What do you observe? Take a few minutes to explore your physical body with this energy; don't rush the process.

You may wish to do this with all your bodies, using the focus points listed below.

Emotional body: Navel and belly area.

Mental body: Forehead and brain area.

Intuitional/compassionate body: Center of the chest.

Will/spirit body: Back and heels.

Soul level: Just below hairline in the middle of the forehead and around the outside of the body.

Divine level: Top of the head.

Eighth level: Breathe into breastbone and sides of chest.

Ninth level: Top of the head and bottom of the feet.

Tenth level: Focus your awareness beyond your body until you feel very light and ask for tenth-level energies.

Eleventh level: Focus your awareness beyond your body until you feel very light and ask for eleventh-level energies.

Twelfth level: Focus on your awareness beyond your body until you feel very light and ask for twelfth-level energies.

Plate 1a   Developed Emotional Aura

Plate 1b   Less Developed Emotional Aura

Plate 2a   Developed Mental Aura

Plate 2b   Less Developed Mental Aura

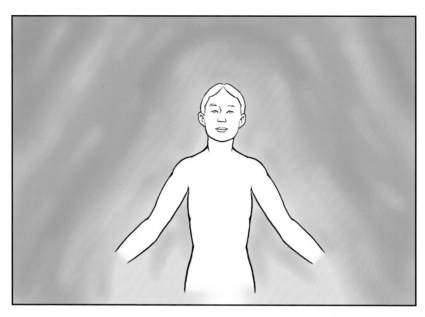

Plate 3 Partially Developed Spiritual Aura

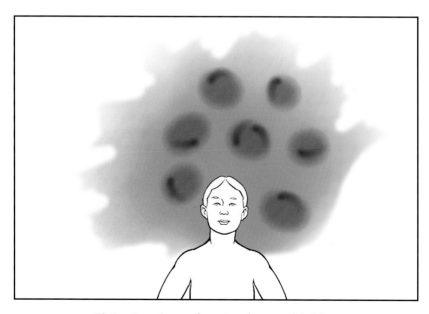

Plate 4 Aura showing heavy thinking

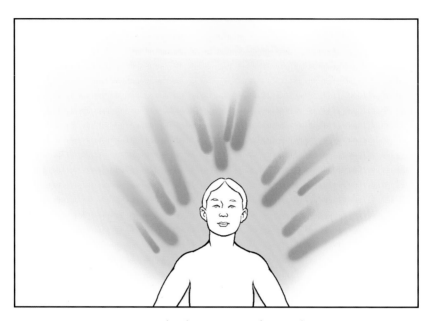

Plate 5   Thinking aura of a meditator

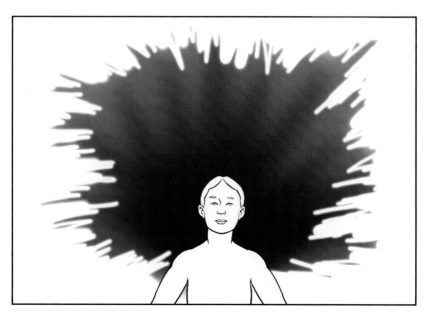

Plate 6   Aura showing fanaticism or blind devotion to an idea, cause, or person

Plate 7a   Unhealthy emotional aura

Plate 7b   Healthy, healing emotional aura

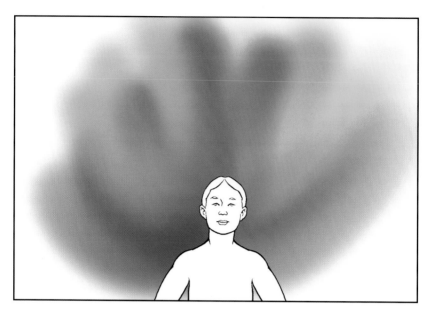

Plate 8   Aura of a person devoted to service in an
action-oriented way

Plate 9   Aura of a person showing anger

Plate 10 Aura of a person in a state of prayer

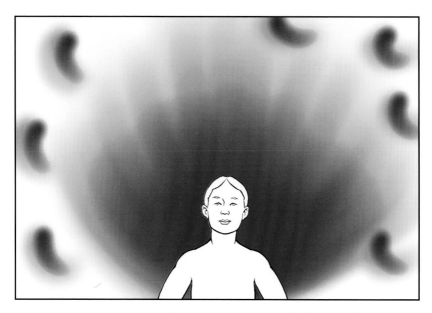

Plate 11 Aura of a person showing feelings of lust

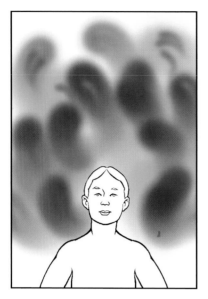

Plate 12 Aura of a
self-centered person who
wants attention

Plate 13 Aura of a person
guided by intuition
and inspiration

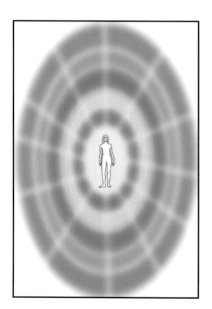

Plate 14 Well Developed
Spiritual Aura

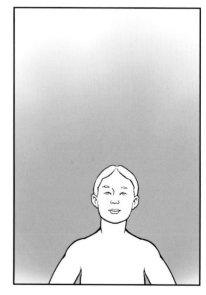

Plate 15 Aura of a
loving person

Meditation 11: Expanding
into Higher States

Be in a meditative state and open the area above the brain stem, including the thalamus, pituitary, and pineal glands. This can be called a transcendent point in our systems. Breathe into the area for a few minutes to help activate it. When you are in touch with the combined energy of the area, fill it with light and expand the energy. You may then:

1. Expand it above your head for about ten feet. Watch your body changes and be aware of any messages that come through or visions that may appear. Sometimes nothing happens at first but peaceful feelings entering your body. Practicing for a few minutes at a time will, however, help open this area to other dimensions and to greater insights.

2. Think of some information you would like as you focus in this area. Answers sometimes take a while to form, but the patience is worth it.

3. Extended practice with this area will help open consciousness. It can sometimes release kundalini, therefore, a person needs to be watchful of this and quit if it seems likely.

4. Send the combined energy to the brains to stimulate them.

5. Focusing in this area can help burn off negativity, which sometimes resides at the top of the brain stem, clouding good use of energy.

Kundalini and Consciousness

Kundalini is an evolutionary force that pushes us into greater consciousness and opens us to spiritual development. Everyone has some already released and active in their system. It's what helps to make a person more intelligent and effective. If more is released, it can increase the effects. However, if a large amount is released and not handled correctly, it can cause problems on any or all levels of the system. For further information, please refer to the author's book, *Kundalini and the Chakras*.

Kundalini can be used in small amounts in meditation by asking some of the already available kundalini to activate the area. When you do this usually a sense of greater alertness and awareness occurs, and the meditations are more effective. It shouldn't be done every day unless you have a kundalini counselor to advise. Occasional use is usually just fine. Too much may release any extra kundalini waiting for a chance to release, which may bring difficulties if your system isn't ready.

Positive and Negative

Sometimes when we are open to a lot of spiritual or positive energy, the universal balance system will also release negativity. If you feel negativity after some very positive experiences that may be what's happening. If so, in a meditative prayer state, ask that all negativity turn to positive as well.

It's a good idea to turn any negativity around you to positive anyway. Then stumbling blocks become positive forces to help you on your path.

Chapter 8

Seven Other Realities

AS OUR CONSCIOUSNESS is pushed further out and further in, we discover there are other realities. Some we already know about and find we are deep into them. Others are just beyond our present grasp, but knocking at the doors of our consciousness. As we add more of these realities to our daily reality, awareness will expand to triple, quadruple, or multidimensional consciousness. The unified theory affects us more already than we know. However, most people still see these realities as "other."

One of the main things to remember is that the energy of all these realities is present in our bodies and consciousness all the time. On occasion, things will happen to give us a peek into these areas. It is easier, however, if we can expand our consciousness outward away from our bodies into a more pure level of consciousness. Then we reach beyond our thoughts, feelings, and blocks. This makes it easier to connect with the vibration of these other realities. Through our intent or will, we can bring the vibrations of a different reality into our bodies, to trigger or awaken what is already there. Once we have done this, it is much easier to awaken these vibrations and develop the use of them.

There are many other realities in addition to the ones with which we are most familiar. In this chapter, we list seven of the realities pressing on the doors of our consciousness. They are the more common, or easily accessed, other realities. We are at a point in our evolution where it is time for these to be incorporated into our daily lives and made usable. The following other realities are:

1. **Akashic Records:** This is the record of our past, present, and possible futures.

2. **Parallel Dimensions:** There are many of them. We will use the one that relates to what will happen on earth.

3. **Time and Space:** Through our consciousness we can go beyond the limitations usually perceived.

4. **Nature:** Nature has incredible power that we can tap into.

5. **Inner Worlds:** This area provides a great strength and healing.

6. **Metaphysics:** This area can go into the very ground of our being.

7. **Mysticism:** This area goes beyond our spiritual life.

Akashic Records

This information is imprinted on the energy called "akasha." It includes your actions, desires, fantasies, hopes, and dreams,

through all of your life and your reactions to them. This information includes past lives, what they were and what they were destined to be; the present as it is and as it is destined to be. The
records contain information regarding a person's evolution. It also
includes the probable futures you have and the destiny purposes
for them.

The records in the akasha have their own energy. If there is an
imbalance any place, it is destined to be balanced in some life or
another. This process of balance is called "karma." Inaction, not
speaking up about what is happening, or not participating in
what's going on around you, can also cause karma.

Through a deep meditative process, sometimes through a
process called psychosynthesis or by a regression into past lives, a
person can change the forces imprinted on the records, which will
bring changes in their present-day situation. It is impossible to
change actual events that have happened; however, attitudes and
other energies can be shifted or modified.

The records can be viewed much as one watches a videocassette
recorder. You can fast forward, reverse, stop, or continue showing
the records, as well as enhance their energies. If what you see in
the records has a dark purple background, it usually means it is
from the past. It usually has a burnished gold background if it is
from the future. Through modifying his or her energy, a person
can actually enter the imprint of the bodies he or she had in a particular life, thus strengthening the awareness and feeling of that
time for greater understanding. The records are continually being
modified by our actions, attitudes, awareness, and intent.

A person's own records also mesh with others' records, especially where group karma is concerned. Historical events can also
imprint your akashic record, especially where it applies to you.
The energy of the akashic records affects the manifestation
process, which in turn affects what happens or doesn't happen to
us. The dream state relates to the manifestation process and whatever is manifesting shows up in dreams first. As we are more in

touch with our dreams, we can help change or modify what will actually happen.

The following meditations may help you understand and work with this energy. Be in a peaceful, relaxed position with your back straight. Lying down may facilitate the meditations as the body is in a more contemplative state.

Meditation 1: Viewing the Akashic Records

Massage the center of your forehead and open that area, letting energy gently flow from it. Get into the feeling of floating and sinking into the floor at the same time. This brings a dual awareness, which will help you retain your present-day consciousness at the same time you view the akashic records.

Fill your body with an indigo or dark purple color. Feel your consciousness open up. Ask to view the record through the center of your forehead. At the same time, open an awareness in your body so you can feel the energy, too.

Watch any pictures you may see, and pay attention to any feelings that may arise. Don't judge them, as that will bring you out of the experience. You may judge them when you have completed the viewing. Let yourself be totally involved in the experience while it is happening so that you get optimum information and understanding from it.

1. Ask the akashic records to show you a specific event or relationship in which you are interested.

2. You may ask the records to show you something from the past that affects something of great importance to you in your life now.

When you have finished, you may wish to make notes so that you can refer to them later. Sometimes more information comes weeks, months, or years afterward.

Stretch well and move around so that you fully get back to the present-day consciousness.

Meditation 2: Becoming Aware of Imprinted Records

Put your consciousness in the center of your forehead, top of your head, behind the end of your breastbone, and behind your navel. Sit quietly for a while as these areas receive your attention. Ask what you are currently imprinting on your records in the akasha.

Let messages, thoughts, or feelings form. Give them plenty of time to come to your consciousness.

Meditation 3: Working with Changes

Put your awareness in the areas listed in Meditation 2.

1. Ask what you need to change for your future. Feel yourself opening up to the changes. Do they feel right for you? Do you feel ready for them? If so, with your intent, bring the new changes into your system.

2. Ask what you are doing well in your life. Becoming aware of what things are going well that can give you great courage and strength to continue. Too often we only find fault with ourselves.

   When we have integrated some of the akashic records with the information from the past, present, and probable futures in our system, life will have more meaning, death less fear, or anxiousness about death, and the sense of our continuity or eternality will be strong.

We will comprehend the importance of balancing karma, developing qualities such as love, endurance, presence in the moment, and others, as well as wanting to help raise the consciousness of the human race. Life is more full and more real in the greater scheme of things.

Parallel Dimensions

There are many parallel dimensions. Some exist at the same time and in our same area, but do not, at the present, affect us very much. However, there is one parallel dimension that affects us heavily, because what we do as a civilization is done there first. Inventions, discoveries, or ideas are completed there first. Through meditation, we can open to this area and receive information on possibilities. If our energy is developed enough, we can tap into this energy at any time. It becomes very usable.

When the energy tries to come into you, it usually makes you very sleepy, or makes you feel as though someone has hit you on the upper forehead. Usually the best way to access this is to bring the energy in through the sixth eye and hypothalamus, let it flood your body, and then let the information form into words, feelings, or pictures. Through this energy, you understand other energy forms and how they can be used. It is also possible to see into storm energy—that is, the energy in the body of a storm—and make changes. This energy can bring a great sense of oneness, fullness and peace.

People who have integrated some of the energy and possibilities of parallel dimensions will live more in tune with greater possibilities, creativity, and productivity. These people are more open to exploring greater depths and heights of life, and are very open to new paths or variations of paths. They generally are not rigid and judgmental. The following exercises hopefully will bring you more in touch with this vast information area.

Meditation 4: Opening
to the Parallel Dimension

Be in a peaceful, relaxed state with your eyes closed. Massage the top of the center of your forehead. Gently let energy flow from it. Be aware of the energy coming from your hypothalamus behind this area. As the energy gently flows out, let it open to form a bowl similar to a satellite dish. As it opens, let energy start to come back into this area and into the hypothalamus. Let it gently fill the area. You may wish to visualize a light rosy pink color with yellow around it.

1. Ask what information, ideas, discoveries, or inventions are there for you.

2. Think of some project in which you are involved, and when you feel in touch with the parallel dimension energies, ask for information regarding your project.

Time, Space, and the Galaxy

There are aspects of time and space beyond our human conceptual abilities. However, as we grow and develop, new awarenesses come to us, including that time and space are vibrations and are changeable. We can and do slow down or speed up time by our attitude toward it. We recognize also that space can be changed and become more usable.

Through understanding time and space, we become more aware of the process of evolution, as well as the energies of our galaxy. The transcendent aspects of time and space are from our galaxy's forces.

Meditation 5: Slowing Time

Ask to feel the vibration of time in your chest area. Then ask it to slow down, aid in this process by slow, peaceful breathing. Expand the vibration of time out the sides of your chest. This will help in the slowing down process, as well as to open you more to the fullness of time.

When we scrunch the time energy in our chests, we have a tendency to dissipate it and then certain things don't seem to happen. We do need to have some forward movement with the time vibration, or nothing will be accomplished.

1. Where in your life have you already spread the time energy out too far sideways and can't seem to get things done? If so, bring some back into your chest for a more forward movement out in front of the chest.

2. When have you scrunched the time vibration so much that you find certain things are not happening for you? (When time is scrunched in your chest a person can feel painful and anxious.)

3. What areas of your life contain a good balance of the fullness of time and the forward movement of time?

4. The above meditations may be done using the head, belly, or solar plexus areas instead.

When you feel like you are overwhelmed by others' energies and you don't have enough space, you can fill your own body with the vibration of space, to help balance energies. Also if you feel you are not connecting enough with others, you may find that you have so much space inside yourself that it is difficult to feel the connections outside of yourself.

Meditation 6: Space

1. Ask the vibration of space to fill your body. Usually a sense of fullness, completeness, and peace fill you as well.

2. Exaggerate the feeling of space within you and let yourself feel arrogant. After experiencing it a few minutes, let it go. This meditation is only so you'll know what not to do! When a person has an exaggerated sense of space (that is, full of himself or herself) and feels arrogant, it can bring anger out in others who want to put that person down, or "burst their balloon."

3. Ask the vibration of space to balance your inside and outside. With a balance, you are aware of yourself and others at the same time. It is a much more comfortable way of relating to others. Also, you may find you don't feel crowded by others.

Meditation 7: Creativity
and the Galactic Energies

New ways of creating become available to us as we open up to these greater energies that come from solar systems and galaxies. It is as though they expand our consciousness way beyond what we have thought possible.

1. Ask your consciousness to open to energies from our galaxy, the Milky Way. Ask for something new you can do with the creativity you are already developing. Ask if there is some new creativity possible for you as you tune into these energies.

2. Ask to tune into the galactic or universal energies and to hear celestial music, celestial wisdom, or be aware of celestial creativity.

3. Ask to be in touch with another solar system. Can you sense how they live and create on planets located there?

Those who have integrated some of the concepts of time and space into their daily consciousness will find they are led to do things at the right time and the right place. Their sense of timing and appropriateness is uncanny. These people will not feel limited by time and space constraints in their daily lives; they will feel freer and more in charge.

Nature

When you open to the vibrations of nature, its power feels many times stronger than what can be felt from water when you are immersed in it. Some people become overwhelmed when they first experience its power, which is stronger at night.

There is a wonderful world of nature spirits, devas, and other beings who inhabit this realm. They know about us. However, with all our intelligence, we are not, as a rule, very aware of them. They would like to work with the human realm in the development of this planet.

Tuning into nature helps us to understand the earth and its purposes, as well as, our purpose for being connected with this planet—the main one being evolution. We understand our own nature better by connecting with earth and its nature.

Meditation 8: Connecting with the Earth

1. Through your feet feel your energy connecting with the earth force. Then let all of your consciousness be attuned to the earth energy. Feel yourself at one with it. Recognize your body's connection with it. It is of earth and needs this connection so that it can function better. We are, however,

of spirit and forget sometimes that our body has a different makeup from us. It is up to us to help in the evolution of the body and its energy while it houses us, and gives us greater opportunity for action and interaction.

2. Ask your body if there are certain vitamins or minerals it needs so that you can bring in pure energy forms, and not have to run the vitamins and minerals through the plant or animal kingdom first.

Meditation 9: Nature Spirits

Be outdoors, preferably in a more rural area or park. Walk around until you find energies quite different from the surrounding areas. Often these contain nature spirits or devas. Sit quietly in this area and let your energies become one with this special place. After you have tuned into this energy by becoming one with it, begin to look around you, slowly and without a strong focus. Sometimes you will be able to see the nature spirits. They do not have the grosser physical bodies which we have; their bodies stop at the etheric stage. Sometimes it is possible to communicate with them through thoughts. It may take a number of times to develop the ability to see and communicate with them, however, it is well worth the effort.

Those in tune with nature will find deep rapport with these energies. Their connectedness with animals and plants will be a joy. These people will probably care deeply for the planet and animals. Some may see nature spirits or have conversational contact with other aspects of nature. People deeply in tune with nature are able to converse with plants, trees, animals, and other forms of nature. They will gain strength and well-being from the earth; they will also be more ecologically minded.

Inner Worlds

Most people never visit this vast area in the depth of their beings, except through depressed or melancholic states. It takes some faith to be able to go into the depths without at first becoming overwhelmed. However, continued work with this area brings great rewards, including great understanding.

Healing is one of the gifts from the inner worlds and is available to all. This is one of the reasons it is said that a person has to "hit bottom" before they can change or be healed. The process of hitting bottom will make the great powers of the inner self available.

Mythical beings exist on these inner levels. All cultures have their myths, many of which are surprisingly similar. Some people see symbols of the mythical beings when exploring the inner world. Understanding can come from viewing these symbols.

Negative influences may be found on this level. One needs to use the protective white light in this instance or cover the negative influence with a white light. We encounter negative influences in our regular daily life as well. It is something we need to learn to handle. Great oneness with God within us is available from here; as is great peace, steadfastness, and other spiritual qualities.

Meditation 10: Opening to Inner Worlds

Focus your attention behind your navel and down about one inch. This area can help you be in touch with the inner worlds through the subconscious area located here. Breathe gently into the area, letting yourself be focused inward.

1. Ask your consciousness to go thirty feet into the inner worlds. (Your system will understand what you mean, even if you don't.) Ask for healing or rejuvenating energies to come from that area into your body. The energy may come in waves.

2. Then go sixty feet inward and ask again for healing and rejuvenation energy.

3. Ask your consciousness to go thirty feet into the inner world. This time ask for any information that is ready for you to come to your awareness.

4. As you are thirty feet into the inner worlds, ask for inner wisdom on some project or concern you may have.

There is nothing magical about thirty or sixty feet. These numbers are used to give you an idea of how far to go in. If there is another number that has personal meaning to you, you may wish to use that. You may find that it is not productive to go much further than the sixty feet in until you are more familiar with this process.

People who are not afraid of their inner worlds or depressions will find they are better able to go into these inner worlds. Benefits of a connection with this area include wisdom, inner strength, healing, and an inner peace. This is the world of shamanism and mythology. Mystics are also at home in this area. For further information, please refer to *Energy-Focused Meditation* by Genevieve Lewis Paulson.

Meditation 11: The Process of Evolution

Our universe is expanding. It's as though what is happening in the universe is also happening in our own private universe. As we touch into the greater or universal expansion it will help us with our own personal growth.

1. Let your consciousness expand out toward the entire universe. Let yourself be aware of the movement, the outward expansion, the opening up.

Then tune into your own system. Is it keeping pace with the universal expansion? Are you behind or pushing too hard with yours? Try to connect with the universal "hum" and let that fill your body, bringing in greater peace and purpose. Be in an open meditation on your growth.

2. Let your consciousness expand and ask to feel the vibrations of other solar systems. Can you sense people located there? What do they seem to be working on in their expansion?

Metaphysics

Webster's dictionary defines metaphysics as "the science that seeks to know the ultimate grounds of being or what it is that really exists." Metaphysics covers a lot of territory and many books have been written on this subject.

For the purposes of this chapter, we concentrate on the part of metaphysics that relates to the expansion of our knowledge and awareness of our makeup and connectedness to others. In our deepest awareness of our makeup, we are aware not only of our bodies, but our connectedness with all others. Once experienced, our view of our creation changes. The following are two meditations to help you to get in touch with these energies.

Meditation 12: Focus on God or Ultimate Energy

Be in a peaceful, meditative state, either sitting or lying down.

1. Extend your consciousness as far out around your body as you can. Imagine it is going many miles beyond you.

2. At the same time, imagine your consciousness is also going many miles deep into your body. This will bring you a dual awareness; beyond and within.

3. Breathe out the sides and front of your chest, in a peaceful, but full, manner.

4. Let your mind be still. Focus on the center of each eyebrow if you can't keep your mind and brains quiet.

5. Focus on God, or whatever you call the Ultimate Energy.

6. Experience the presence of God or Ultimate Energy in your entire self. Feel the connection of that energy with yours.

7. Be in an open meditation and let your thoughts and feelings process the information.

Meditation 13: Cells and the Cosmos

Follow steps 1 through 5 of the above meditation.

6. Focus on your cells. Ask to feel the individuality of each of your cells.

7. Go deeper into the awareness and ask to experience the touch of the cosmos present in each cell.

8. After experiencing the cell and cosmos energies for a few minutes, ask to feel the connectedness of your system with that of others.

9. Be in an open meditation and let your thoughts and feelings process the information.

Those who have integrated energies from this area into their daily lives will see meaning in all things. They will also see the interconnectedness of all things. These people are not bound by what things seem to be, as they understand there are many levels of any incident or situation; they have greater control of life through the understanding and use of energies.

Mysticism

As well as being pushed into the above-mentioned other realities, through spirit and development of greater consciousness we are being pushed into spiritual dimensions beyond our usual areas. Some of the things that will happen through discovery and use of these higher realms are:

- Greater powers, sometimes called *Siddhis,* which will give us superhuman powers.

- Gift of words, which will bring more inspired speaking, writing, and creating, is available from these higher spiritual dimensions.

- Greater oneness with God—beyond the self. It is wonderful (full of wonder) when one balances this with the sense of God within from the inner worlds.

- A sense of the spiritual purposes of evolution.

In the mystical realm, mysteries and miracles are understood. Also, we are more able to do things that are called miracles by others.

Meditation 14: Mystical Levels

1. Breathe deeply and peacefully into your system, until you feel as though you have touched your very core.

2. Keeping the above feeling, expand some of your energies outward beyond your body until you feel

as though you have made a connection with the divine level in outer space.

3. Feel the energies of the inner and outer spaces together and let them feel balanced, giving extra energy to whichever one needs it.

4. Ask to feel God (or whatever you call that energy) deep within you. Then ask to feel God beyond you. Feel the balance and fullness.

5. Ask to be in touch with mystical levels. What mysteries, secrets, or deep wisdom is there for you?

Meditation 15: Exploring the Combination

Follow steps 1 through 3 above.

4. Ask to feel joy or bliss in these areas.

5. Feel thankfulness and appreciation.

6. Be in awe of these energies and then become one with them.

7. Be in an open meditation, making yourself available to other experiences from this level.

Those people who have integrated this area into their daily lives will have a great, profound connection with God or whatever they call that energy. It does not matter what your religious choice is, when the mystical levels are attained. They usually have spiritual gifts such as healing, deep intuition, and compassion, as well as other gifts. The oneness with the Divine is also a daily blessing. Hidden messages are clear.

Some people have natural gifts in some of these areas, which blossom with understanding and development. Each person's abilities depend also on how conducive their paths are to these energies and how much effort they are willing to put into their development. There are many other gifts and attributes from each of these levels that are not mentioned here. If you wish to expand into twelve other realities, there are five that many people are already exploring, including: (1) the realm of the angels; (2) the realm of guides; (3) the realm of the deceased; (4) the myriad of beautiful heavens or higher levels of luminous intensity; and (5) the great void.

Evolution is Pushing Us

There is no way we can remain with the same intelligence, consciousness, and capabilities as we have in the past. The energy affecting us is relentlessly pushing us into these greater, more expanded ways of being. We are being forced to be a part of a quantum leap in evolution. Most people living at this time have consciously chosen to incarnate at this time because of the extra power for growth.

It is necessary to take some conscious control of how the changes are going to affect each of us. We need to be cocreators in our own evolution. Otherwise, we will find ourselves pushed into heavy or strange situations from which we will have to emerge from by using our new powers. Those who live in the expanded consciousness, which comes from integrating other realities such as these listed, will find new ways of being. These new ways are more creative, productive, and enlightened. The choices in life are so much greater than before. It is a wonderful way of being.

Chapter 9

The Spherical System

THERE ARE MANY different energy systems and forces in our bodies, and the spherical system, though little-known, is one of the more fascinating ones. However, when you work with these energies, you usually recognize the feelings. Israel Regardie, in *The Middle Pillar*, refers to some of these spheres, and their energy is referred to in *Tibetan Yoga and the Secret Doctrine,* edited by W. Y. Evans-Wentz. He mentions attributes of some of the spheres and their locations. He does not refer to them, however, as spheres.

The more developed spheres relate to what may be called transcendent or paranormal abilities. Full development of these abilities can take years. Some development occurs naturally in people who have achieved certain levels of growth, either through being born with higher

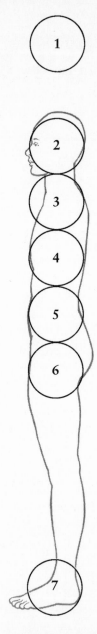

Figure 9.1 Locations of the Seven Spheres

1—the Higher Self Sphere; 2—the Head Sphere; 3—the Neck Sphere; 4—the Heart Sphere; 5—the Subconscious Sphere; 6—the Kundalini Sphere; 7—the Feet Sphere

energies, or through their spiritual growth work. Some of the gifts of the areas also can appear spontaneously. However, full development requires the intent or focus of the individual.

The spheres are activated by a combination of prana, sexual energy, and earth energy focused in a particular "battery" area. These may be called psychic batteries, and are formed by a concentration of an energy that vibrates at a particular rate. When this happens spontaneously, it can cause blockages or heaviness in the body until the energies are put to work, usually through conscious intent or focus. One does need to interact with this process.

This system contains seven etheric spheres (see Figure 9.1 at left). They interconnect, and actually help power one another. If one is blocked or slowed down, all others will be affected, too. They work separately but also in unison or sometimes in combinations. Uses for the spheres are:

1—The Higher Self Sphere

The high spiritual and soul level energies form the basis for the psychic battery in this area. Its uses include: transforming one's consciousness into the higher states, being a connection between self and soul, bringing direction from soul to the personality, and bringing vitality and healing to the individual.

2—The Head Sphere

The high mental and spiritual energy found in the area below the corpus callosum bridge (involving the pineal, pituitary, and hypothalamus areas), form the energy for the psychic battery in this area. Its uses include: very high awareness, seeing things through a radiant light, understanding beyond human awareness, and recognizing the spiritual levels.

3—The Neck Sphere

The will is the battery power here. This sphere deals with choice, action, mental power, and control. It gives power to our actions.

4—The Heart Sphere

The love energy found in the heart area (center of the chest) forms the energy for the psychic battery in this sphere. Its uses are for love, motivation, profoundness, and deep creativity.

5—The Subconscious Sphere

The energy found in the subconscious area forms the energy for the psychic battery. Its uses include: warming the body *(tumo)*, healing, and bringing the collective unconscious energies into awareness.

6—The Kundalini Sphere

Kundalini forms the energy for the psychic battery. The uses of this energy are for body strength, especially the lower body, cooling of the system, earth wisdom, and expression, especially through words.

7—The Feet Sphere

Earth energy forms the battery for this sphere. Some of the uses are healing, body strength, endurance, earth connection, and public speaking.

The spheres are different sizes in different people, depending on how much a person focuses on, and uses, a sphere. Although they are generally round, they can have an oval shape.

Their energy can also expand quite beyond their normal size when activated. Your life purpose would indicate which ones would develop the most. However, as a part of your overall development, they all need to be activated and usable. You may have a particular sphere well developed, and then not use it for a long period of time. It would then tend to shrink, and in some cases, the energy could turn negative. Especially if the energy backs up into the physical body, health problems could occur. Even if you do not use a previously developed sphere, the potential for its use is still there. You cannot discern a person's development by the size of the sphere.

Problems through our lives spur growth in these areas. However, if the growth is not achieved, then the incident or situation instead leaves an undigested energy, which will continue to surface and inhibit other growth. This chapter includes information for cleansing the spheres, aiding in their greater use and development.

Usually the spheres are filled with many memories, attitudes, and blocks from previous lives, as well as the current one. Sometimes fear of the future may also leave blocks in these areas. To get the maximum benefit from these areas, and not to cause trouble with the system by trying to do higher work through the mud and mire, it is very important to cleanse the spheres before developing them for higher use. The following pages outline a cleansing process that can help speed the development process and make the spheres more usable. Greater psychic and spiritual development can occur when the spheres are cleaned. Some people like to repeat the cleansing process periodically as new things surface. In the section following the cleansing procedures, information will be given on activating these spheres as well as exercises for their use.

Figure 9.1 shows the location of the seven spheres used in this cleansing procedure. Note: The higher self sphere is located in the space above the head, equal to the person's height.

Cleansing the Spheres

The spheres cannot reach their potential as far as gifts or powers if they are full of blocked energy. The blocks could be undigested experiences and memories. By undigested, we mean learning and growth hasn't been achieved, so the experiences and memories linger like undigested food in the system. Actually, experiences and memories are food for our growth and development.

Going through the process of cleansing is a fascinating journey into one's past, in the current life, as well as previous lives. People usually feel much freer and better able to function in their world.

For some, the change is immediate. For others, the greatest improvement comes two or three weeks after the cleansing.

Cleansing Procedure

The cleansing procedures are the same for each one. It is usually best to start the cleansing process with the subconscious sphere since it affects the entire spherical system the strongest for most people—it can be very stubborn and pushy!

With this spherical system we show four sections, or quadrants. However, if a person wishes each of the quadrants can be divided into three sections making a total of twelve. We use the four quadrant system as most people become overloaded on the twelve quadrant system. Either way, when doing the cleansing, if something comes through that is very heavy and not easily worked with, one should fill that area with the color lavender to heal it, and then take the information to a qualified counselor to explore further. Walking, dancing, and swimming are all ways of helping to keep the energy flowing in these spheres.

You will note the numbering sequence is not the same for each, that is, the pattern alternates. This is due to the circular motion of the spheres and the energy flow as depicted in Figures 9.2 and 9.11.

Subconscious Cleansing

The subconscious is what we call the physical/emotional consciousness. It was never meant to be subconscious or below our consciousness, however, as the mental abilities and consciousness developed this physical/emotional level was not used as much. People began to shut off their feelings, and in so doing, contact with the physical/emotional level was lessened. When one closes off this area, good contact and awareness is lost. This physical/emotional level becomes "subconscious." It never ceased to operate, however, and still influences much of what we do or say to help gets its message across. Everything we do is affected one way or another by the subconscious. Sometimes it agrees and reinforces what we are

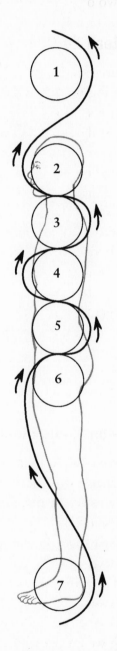

Figure 9.2 Upward Flow Cleansing the Spheres

going to do. Other times its energies are programmed another way and it will therefore block any action it can.

Usually the more mental a person is, the more the physical/emotional responses are ignored or blocked. By conscious effort, you can open this area and have expanded consciousness in your life. In order to do this, you must be able to change the vibratory energy from mental to physical/emotional and back again. Some people are able to maintain a dual awareness of these two levels with quite interesting results. Those who do not use their mental energy very much are usually more naturally open to the physical/emotional levels.

Everyone gets into situations or relationships that trigger memories and blocks from the subconscious. This is a way of understanding how to work with these energies. Some people will have visions, dreams, songs, or other messages coming from the subconscious when it is upset about something. For instance, if my subconscious is upset about dangerous terrain, physical or otherwise, the song "To a Wild Rose" will go through my head. The wild rose is the state flower of North Dakota (my birthplace and home for my first seventeen years), and the song refers to the very flat terrain, with no mountains or dangerous roads. (At one time North Dakota had the record of the longest stretch of an absolutely straight road in the country.) In other words, my subconscious is longing for safer territory, and I know that I need to be more careful and watchful, or at least to recognize its fears. It then does not put up blocks to what I am doing because I have heard it with my mental energies and worked with it.

Opening Dialogue

Past lives, the past in this life, the present, and memory of the future all affect the subconscious energy. It has its own thought processes and does not change willingly. Usually what we think or reason on the mental level does not reach the subconscious area—

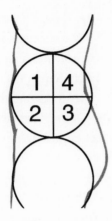

Figure 9.3
The Subconscious Sphere

Figure 9.4 The Sphere is divided into 12 sections, 3 to a quadrant.

it is in a totally different vibrational level. Communication can be achieved between the two, but one has to consciously work for the opening of, and connection to, the two vibratory levels. The following method of cleansing is one way of achieving the connection and opening up some dialogue as well as you release old, nonviable energies.

Whether a person will feel immediate changes after a cleansing, or the changes take two to three weeks to complete themselves, there is always immediate understanding of inner driving forces that may not have been known previously. A lavender color is used throughout this exercise for its healing qualities.

The Spheres and Their Sections

The figure above shows the subconscious sphere and its location (see Figure 9.3), looking like a wheel. However, it is a sphere full of energy. This sphere continually moves and is powered by connection with other spheres, which we will study later. This sphere is made up of etheric energy vibrating on the physical/emotional level. It can be felt more easily than seen. One would have to have good etheric sight in order to see it, and then would also be able to see energy blocks or unbalanced patterns.

If this energy sphere gets blocked, or slowed down, it can cause too much inappropriate energy released into the system, which can then cause physical problems. They may manifest as digestion problems or lower back pains. It also affects one's decision making process and behavior patterns.

The sphere empties its thoughts primarily at the front, so you continually have some input from this area. However, since it is in continual revolution, unless heavily blocked, something comes from different sections each time. In times of excessive excitement, it can go too fast, thus pouring out more than can be easily handled. Most people are unaware of this process. It is something like a washing machine, continually showing different clothes at the top as it turns. However, after you have worked with these energies, great awareness of the process and content can be achieved. You will note that the location for the subconscious is in the belly area. There is also a place in the brain that relates to the subconscious, and that of course if very important in your energy as well. However, for working on the subconscious area, the belly location is most effective.

The four sections are much like four sections of an orange. By doing the four sections instead of the twelve mentioned before, the most important information from each area surfaces and can be dealt with in an easier fashion. There is nothing wrong with doing the twelve levels other than the possibility that the person's energy and attention level is not enough to carry it through. (If someone is leading the exercise, his or her energies may wane as well.)

Subconscious Cleansing Procedure

It is much easier to practice a cleansing if someone else leads it. The person going through the cleansing is better able to focus on the information if someone is guiding them. Some people, however, are able to work solo on cleansings, and do them very well. If you cleanse by yourself, notes can be made during the procedure.

It is usually very helpful if the person leading the cleansing keeps notes for several reasons. It lets the leader remember where he or she is in the process and it can form the basis for the person going on the cleansing to focus for further study. Tape recording the entire procedure is also a good idea. The record keeping should not be used as a thorough record of the entire procedure, but only to remember key information.

This is a fairly easy procedure, as the subconscious desperately wants to be acknowledged in our lives, and willingly enters into the process. On occasion it will be sullen or angry and noncooperative, but not usually. The following are some things of which to be aware:

1. Never leave one sphere only partially done. The unfinished sections may open by themselves. If you can't finish the sphere, fill the other areas with lavender and blessings, otherwise it will feel lopsided.

2. The leader should focus also on the area being cleansed in order to help energies manifest their information.

3. Read cleansing steps 1 through 5 listed below, to understand the process well.

4. Watch for blocking. Sometimes a person hits a superficial area and needs to breathe peacefully, but deeply, in order to go to a more real level and get better information.

5. There are seldom the same incidents from one area since the energy is continually moving. Also, if the energy is truly released, something else will come up.

6. Always look for learning. Keep it positive that way.

7. You may wish to make copies of the Spherical Cleansing Chart to use (see Appendix, page 197), or make up your own.

Cleansing

The person going on the cleansing should be lying down in a comfortable position, usually flat on his or her back, with perhaps a small pillow. A bigger pillow usually blocks energy flow.

The person can prepare by taking deep, peaceful breaths, focusing on the first quadrant (see Figure 9.3). The area is made more easily accessible by breathing into it. The person may also want to feel full in that area as that will help to focus consciousness in there.

1. Ask to see a color or colors. You may see, or sense, them. Asking for colors accomplishes several things. One, it's easier to focus in on the prevailing energy of the section and, two, the color will help bring further information to consciousness through resonance with the event or events housed in the particular area.

2. Let your mind ramble and watch thoughts, feelings, or pictures that appear, and then share them with the leader. If you are doing the cleansing alone, make notes regardless of how unimportant they may seem to be at the time, or talk into a tape recorder.

3. After becoming aware of your thoughts, feelings, or pictures, the leader should ask if the seed incident (the original happening) occurred in this or a past life.

   a. If it is a past life. . .

      . . . Ask if you were a male or female in that life.

      . . . Ask if you were young, middle-aged, or old when this incident happened. Then watch and experience what had happened.

   b. If the seed incident is from this life, re-experience it for greater understanding and to release it.

      (Note: The reason for asking the information in steps "a" and "b" is that knowledge gives you a stronger connection to the life.)

4. After listening to the seed incident, the leader should ask you what you learned and how that affects your life today.

   a. If the incident was negative, fill the area with a lavender color to heal and erase it. Ask the lavender for a message on how to use this energy in the future.

   b. If the situation is a positive one, then the area may be filled with radiant light to enhance it. Sometimes it is also helpful to spread the energy of the good incident combined with the radiant light all over the body.

5. It is good to fill the quadrant with thanks or appreciation after the cleansing as this completes the process. Also, these areas like to be thanked and appreciated.

We will now start with the feet sphere, and work through the system, ending with the higher self sphere. You should try to do spheres seven through one. However, the first time it is much easier to do the subconscious one first.

Some people only like to go through the cleansing of one sphere at a time. That can be helpful in that it gives a person more time to process and adjust to the new release of energy. If you adjust to the energy changes more slowly, pausing between steps can be helpful.

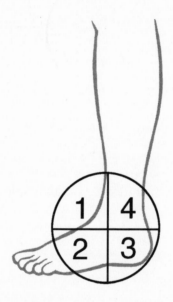

Figure 9.5 The Feet Sphere

The Feet Sphere

The feet sphere relates to earth, confidence, body strength, and also transforms much healing energy from earth to be used in the body. One sphere (see Figure 9.5, above) covers both feet. Also use the Spherical Cleansing Chart in the Appendix, and the cleansing steps listed on page 152 for this sphere.

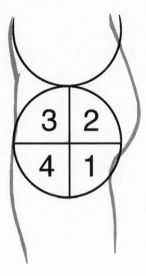

Figure 9.6 The Kundalini Sphere

The Kundalini Sphere

The cleansing of this sphere (see Figure 9.6) may release kundalini that may be stuck there. If this happens, it is best to stop the procedure and let the kundalini rise up above the top of your head. Then it should mix with divine energy and shower over your entire body. After resting a few moments, the cleansing can be continued. However, if the kundalini is too rampant, then, after rising and showering, the kundalini area should be filled with lavender until you feel calm, and then end the procedure. Usually, when this sphere is opened, it helps power the others. Again, use the Spherical Cleansing Chart in the Appendix, and the cleansing steps listed on page 152.

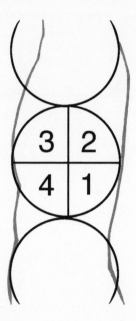

Figure 9.7 The Heart Sphere

The Heart Sphere

The energy of this sphere (see Figure 9.7), as would be expected, has information on relationships. It also sometimes has information on how you live your life: fully, passionately, or pulled back and not entering into opportunities. The cleansing process is the same for this sphere, except note the first quadrant is located in a different place from where the subconscious is located. Use the Spherical Cleansing Chart in the Appendix, and the cleansing steps listed on page 152.

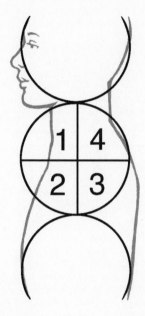

Figure 9.8 The Neck Sphere

The Neck Sphere

The energy of this sphere (see Figure 9.8) relates to the use of will and how it accepts life and makes choices. Much stubbornness can come from here. Again, use the Spherical Cleansing Chart in the Appendix, and the cleansing steps listed on page 152 for this sphere.

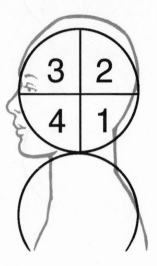

Figure 9.9 The Mental Sphere

The Mental Sphere

The energy in this sphere relates more to the attitudes and perceptions you have rather than feelings or emotions. It helps determine how you want to structure your life. Prejudices, desires, a sense of what is appropriate for one's hoped for lifestyle, are all part of this sphere's contents. The cleansing work is the same as the others. Please note the first quadrant is where the subconscious one is located. (See Figure 9.9). The Spherical Cleansing Chart can be used for this sphere as the process is the same as explained in the subconsciousness cleansing area. Follow the cleansing steps listed on page 152.

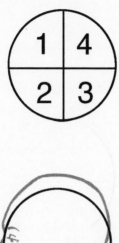

Figure 9.10 The Higher Self (Spiritual) Sphere

The Higher Self (Spiritual) Sphere

The higher self, or spiritual sphere (see Figure 9.10) is above the head. The distance above the top of the head to this sphere is usually equal to the height of the person. When doing this cleansing, knowing the exact distance isn't that necessary as your focus will usually line up correctly through intent. That is, if you are focused on the particular vibration of the higher self sphere, the consciousness will automatically go there. The cleansing procedure is the same as for the others. It is interesting to note that some of the information given by this sphere can be very direct and, sometimes, sharp. Again, the Spherical Cleansing Chart in the Appendix, and the cleansing steps listed on page 152 are to be used.

Complete Flow

When all spheres are reasonably clean, so that they can rotate, energy can automatically flow around and between them. This causes a complete flow of energy (see Figures 9.2 and 9.11), which vitalizes the spheres. This helps them function.

The feet, subconscious, neck, and higher self spheres rotate in the direction of the upper back of the sphere to the front of the sphere. The kundalini, heart, and mental spheres rotate in the direction of the lower front to the back of the sphere.

Focusing on bringing the complete flow around the spheres helps the process. It also helps the spheres keep their rotating process. The complete flow of energy begins with earth energy, and picks up the energy of other spheres as it goes along. When the flow is completed, the combination of energies goes into the earth.

Meditation 1: Complete Flow

After cleansing all spheres, you may wish to do the complete flow. However, it may be done separately, and not just after a cleansing. If the kundalini sphere cleansing is overpowering, the complete flow may help balance the energy.

Lie down flat on your back, without a pillow under the head (under your knees is fine). Then proceed as follows:

1. View Figure 9.2 on page 147 to understand the upward flow.

2. Visualize or sense the feet sphere rotating from the front, under the feet, up the back, and up to the kundalini sphere.

3. Visualize or sense the kundalini sphere as rotating from the back part, underneath, and up the front.

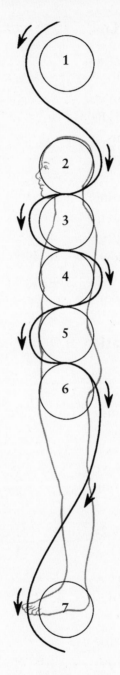

Figure 9.11 Downward Flow Cleansing the Spheres

4. The energy should then go up, back, and over the subconscious sphere. At the top of this sphere, visualize or sense the energy flowing to the bottom of the heart sphere, going under it and up the front.

5. At the top, visualize or sense the energy going under and up the back of the neck sphere.

6. At the top of this sphere, visualize or sense the energy going up to the mental sphere. Let the energy go under and up the front.

7. Visualize or sense the energy going up the back of the higher self sphere and over the top.

8. At the top, let the energy go down the front (see Figure 9.11) and continue down all spheres in reverse of how it came up. When you reach the bottom of the feet sphere, let the energy gently connect with where it started.

9. Be at peace for about five or ten minutes and let any thoughts or feelings that you wish come to your awareness.

10. Stretch well before rising.

11. Review the experience to ascertain whether the flow was even. If not, breathing into the uneven area and filling it with lavender can help balance energies. Take time to review the process and see if there is anything else you need from the exercise.

Chapter 10

Developing the Spheres

All of the spheres need seven forces in order to be used for higher purposes. They may be considered paranormal uses since they are beyond our usual capacity for expression. These seven forces are:

1. Prana
2. Sexual energy
3. Earth energy
4. The "battery" power of the particular sphere
5. Conscious intent (meditation focus)
6. Rhythm
7. Appropriate color, to enhance the process (optional)

1. Prana

Prana is a basic life force, which comes from the sun. We breathe it into our bodies, as well as receive it through our skin. There are many levels of prana, and usually the vibration of the area on which one is focusing will attract the proper level of prana.

2. Sexual Energy

Sexual energy is something everyone has, even if the person is not in touch with it, or it feels dormant. It comes from the genital area, and is a very powerful force that can transmute into many different forms. Some of these are: healing, greater mental ability, rejuvenation, joy of life, and spiritual awakening, to name a few. Some people choose not to be sexually involved in order to save this energy for other meditative and higher consciousness work. If the energy is not readily available for meditation, a person may ask their etheric level sexual energy to flow instead. (Etheric level is a higher level of the physical body.)

3. Earth Energy

Earth energy also has a number of forms and uses. For these exercises, we ask for earth energy to come up through our feet to the particular sphere activated at the time.

4. Psychic Batteries

These areas are called psychic batteries because they power psychic abilities. They come from a concentration of a particular vibration of energy located in the sphere. The spheres and their batteries are:

Sphere 1: Earth

Sphere 2: Kundalini

Sphere 3: Subconscious

Sphere 4: Love

Sphere 5: Will

Sphere 6: Mind

Sphere 7: Spiritual and soul

5. Conscious Intent

Conscious intent is a very important part of the process. It sets the energy into productivity. If you do not add your conscious intent, the energies of the sphere will still be there and tend to cause discomfort. Also, the possibilities will not come to fruition without the input of conscious intent. Sometimes a teacher or facilitator can add her or his conscious intent to get things moving. This is the process which helps the cleansing listed in the previous section to be accomplished.

6. Rhythm

Rhythm gives us balance and movement. Anything that brings rhythm into the energy, such as breathing rhythmically or feeling rhythm in your body, can help. Sometimes, listening to drums or other percussion instruments rhythmically played can work, too.

Israel Regardie in his book, *The Middle Pillar*, writes, "There could hardly be a better adjunct than breathing in a rhythmical manner." Breathing rhythmically may be done by breathing in for two through six, or eight counts, holding the breath for the count chosen, breathing out with the count and holding also for the count. You may wish to try different numbers to see which feels best. Some people use their pulse rate to set the beat. Some, however, can fall into a rhythm pattern just by thinking about it. Their breathing then adjusts to the rhythm.

7. Color

Colors imagined or seen in the spheres is helpful as it accentuates the energy. If the colors are a distraction, don't use them.

Kundalini

Kundalini is basic evolutionary energy and, as such, it affects your entire life. This spherical system is not dependent on the kundalini except as the battery for the kundalini sphere. When flowing well and usable in our system, it enhances everything we do. When a person specifically adds kundalini to other energies, it can do the following:

1. Increase the power.

2. Increase your awareness or consciousness.

3. Raise the energies to higher levels or octaves.

As a part of the meditations, kundalini will sometimes be used as well.

How to Know a Sphere is Releasing

Spheres can be triggered by astrological combinations, achieving special spiritual levels, or through spiritual practice. If you are not developed enough to use it, you may feel exhausted, unable to function well or at all, and your body may feel weird or numb.

There are a variety of symptoms which show up when a sphere is opening on its own. The following are some effects that may alert you:

1. A particular sphere may have a rumbling or swirling feel, which can be exciting or scary. If it is in one of the two lower ones it may affect digestion or cause diarrhea.

2. You may be filled with inertia and unable to focus on what you are trying to do.

3. Your energy and consciousness may be muddled in a particular sphere, which is trying to activate, thus leaving you feeling confused and out of sync.

4. You may feel that "something is about to happen," because of the intensity of the energy.

What to Do if a Sphere Activates by Itself

When a sphere activates itself, you can focus on it, fill it with lavender, and ask the sphere what it wants to do or how it wants to be used. It is helpful to remain very quiet while the sphere is activating or the process will slow down, and you may feel heavy. Sometimes exaggerating the energy can help it release and open it up. It does need your conscious awareness and intent to really work well. When one has a tendency towards activation of the spheres, it can happen at any time or place.

Activating the Spheres

The minimum results from activating these spheres is a more balanced system, with better energy flows, feelings of peacefulness, and well-being. Obviously, the more you work with these spheres, the greater the development of these almost superhuman abilities. All spheres should be worked with in order to keep a balance within the system. However, each sphere does not need to be worked at the same time.

There are openings on each sphere (see Figure 10.1, following page), which are focus points for action. Attention should be focused there as well as the center of the sphere, as that helps facilitate the action.

Feet Sphere

1. Battery Source: earth

2. Purpose:

   - Help us be connected to, and conscious of, the earth.

   - Brings strength and consciousness from the earth to help us walk fast and remain surefooted.

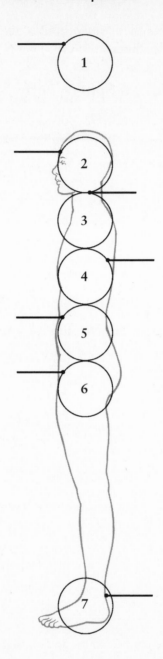

Figure 10.1 Openings in the Spheres

- Receives nurturing from earth.

- Brings energy from earth to the body so it can handle the higher spiritual energies well.

- Helps in public speaking.

3. Negative side, when closed:

- You can feel disconnected and alienated, your body, insecure.

- It's easier to become ill or to be overwhelmed by cosmic energies.

- Your feet may be swollen, feel excessively warm, or hurt.

4. Meditations for Development

Preparation for Meditation

  a. Focus on your feet, feeling the sphere as large enough to include both feet. As you focus on this area, feel the energy of the "battery" of the earth energy.

  b. Visualize or feel prana coming into the area.

  c. Visualize or feel sexual energy coming into the area.

  d. Bring more earth energy into the sphere.

  e. Fill the area with a copper color.

  f. Breathe in a rhythmic manner.

  g. Focus on the activating point.

Meditation 1: Connection
with the Earth

1. Ask the combined energy to open to the earth and connect with it.

2. Let the connection with earth bring you greater awareness of the earth. Be in an open meditation and see what information or awarenesses come to you.

3. Ask to feel the nurturing earth energies coming into this sphere, and then into your entire body.

Meditation 2: Walking

Do this exercise when walking to help increase sure-footedness, and increase your speed. You may feel very light in your feet.

Meditation 3: Public Speaking

Imagine you are standing in front of an audience, giving a speech. Feel energy from the earth go into the feet sphere and up through your body, with some going from your heart, and the top of your head, to the audience. Also let some of the energy go out your mouth to the audience. Then visualize the energy going through the audience back into earth and then over to you. Repeat the process. This forms an oval of energy that makes speaking easy and dynamic, and connects the speaker and the audience. It's best to practice this a few times before actually using it.

Kundalini Sphere

1. Battery Source: Kundalini

2. Purpose:

- Body strength.

- When open, it opens up sciatic nerve, legs, and entire lower region.

- Affects intestines (as does subconscious).

- Help to raise body to a higher level.

- Runners and athletes perform better with this sphere open.

- Wisdom, especially when connected to the heart sphere. "Fly by the seat of the pants." Opens the ability to comprehend.

- Words—better able to communicate, especially when connected to the throat sphere.

- Cooling the body.

- Transformation.

- Release of kundalini.

3. Negative side, when closed:

- Can cause diarrhea when not functioning properly.

- Tenses sciatica, leg areas and brings maladies to that region.

4. Recognizing when activated:

- Energy rumbles in the sphere, sometimes making you feel as though the bottom is dropping out.

5. Meditations for Development:

Preparation for Meditation

a. Focus on the area between the anus and the genitals, the home of the kundalini energy. As you focus on this area, if too much energy is released expand it into the sphere. If it still feels strong, you may wish to skip the focus in this area and move to step "b."

b. Visualize or feel prana coming into the area.

c. Visualize or feel sexual energy coming into the sphere.

d. Bring earth energy into the sphere.

e. If the area feels strong, fill it with a white light, otherwise an orange color is fine.

f. Breathe in a rhythmic manner.

g. Focus on the activating point.

Meditation 4: Helping the Body

1. Focus on the kundalini sphere and ask its energy to go into the entire body to strengthen it.

2. Vary this exercise by asking that the strengthening energy release tensions on the sciatic nerves, and in your legs.

3. Vary this exercise by imaging you are doing physical exercises or work with help from the energy of this sphere. Then when you are actually exercising or working, again ask for this help.

4. Vary this exercise by asking the energy to strengthen and heal the intestinal area. This can also help give you "intestinal fortitude."

5. Ask the energy of this level to transform your body energy to a higher level, so spiritual energies are easier to receive.

Meditation 5: Wisdom

1. Think of a problem while focusing on this area. Be in an open meditation and see if problem-solving information comes through.

2. Imagine yourself doing things and ask for the energy of "flying by the seat of your pants" to help you.

3. Meditate on this sphere and ask for information on how to improve your communication.

Meditation 6: Transformation

1. Ask the energy of this sphere to transform your negative energies to positive.

2. Ask the energies of this sphere to transform your sexual energies to a creative or spiritual level.

3. Ask the energies of this sphere to cool your body. (This is the opposite of tumo, which warms the body.)

Meditation 7: Raising Kundalini

We do not recommend doing this meditation unless you have had prior kundalini work, or are under the guidance of a qualified kundalini teacher, as it may release too much, too soon, and, perhaps, not flow well through the body and out the top of the head. Further information may be found in *Kundalini and the Chakras,* by this author.

Focus on the energy of the sphere and the kundalini area located between the anus and the genitals. Ask energy of the sphere to activate the kundalini. With your thoughts, raise the kundalini up the spine and out the top of the head. Let it mix with divine energy and shower back around and in you. Spend a few minutes in open meditation.

Subconscious Sphere

1. Battery Source: Subconscious

2. Purpose:

- To develop tumo (psychic heat), used to:

    a. Bring heat into the body and warm the area around the body. Some people are able to warm large areas.

    b. Bring healing into the body.

    c. Rejuvenate the body.

    d. Help the body be supple, by dancing with it.

    e. Strengthen and relax the body.

- Develop powerful energies, which can be used to:

    a. Help visualize new ways of doing things.

    b. Bring a special, almost magical energy into whatever you do.

- Develop energy through working with *nadis* (etheric nerve-like connections throughout the system), which can be used to:

    a. Fire the nadis, to make you more energetic, magnetic, and radiant.

    b. Putting light into the nadis to bring more spiritual energy.

- Develop brain energy, which can be used to:

    a. Expand consciousness and awareness.

    b. Strengthen the brain power.

- Develop spiritual energy, which can be used to:

    a. Deepen meditative states.

    b. Enhance happiness, joy, and bliss.

    c. Help release kundalini.

3. Negative side, when closed:

- May bring nausea, diarrhea.
- Can make you too upset to function well.

- May rumble in your lower abdominal area, and bring a feeling of impending change

4. Meditations for Development

Preparations for Meditation

a. Focus on the area behind the navel and down about an inch and a half. As you focus on this area, feel the energy of the "battery," the subconscious energy in this sphere.

b. Visualize or feel prana coming into the area.

c. Visualize or feel sexual energy coming into the area.

d. Bring earth energy up through the feet into the area.

e. Fill the area with a lavender color.

f. Breathe in a rhythmic manner.

g. Focus on the activating point.

Meditation 8: Developing the Tumo

Note: In the following exercises, only hold the energy for about three to five minutes in the beginning, until your system adjusts to it. After that use your own discretion. (It's best not to overdo it.)

1. Ask the combined energy in the area to turn to heat (tumo). Expand the heat over your entire body. When the body is warm, discontinue the exercise.

2. Ask the tumo to turn to a healing energy and fill the entire body. Then send the energy to any particular area of the body.

3. Ask the tumo to turn to a rejuvenating energy and fill the entire body.

4. Ask the tumo to fill the entire body, and then dance freeform for a few minutes.

5. Ask the tumo to turn to strength and relaxation in the body.

Meditation 9: Developing the Powerful Energies

Focus on this sphere and ask for its energies to bring power and strength to your entire body. Then stretch or dance with this energy in order to assimilate it and make it usable.

Meditation 10: Developing Energy with Nadis

Nadis are similar to nerves, located in the etheric body. There are hundreds of them and they are important in the functions of the etheric body.

Let yourself be light and ethereal. Ask the energy of this sphere to be fire-like and to go into the nadis and empower them. Ask the nadis to be more energetic, magnetic, and radiant.

Vary this exercise by asking the energy from this sphere to turn to light in the nadis in order to bring in more spiritual energy.

Meditation 11: Developing Brain Energy

1. Ask the energy of this sphere to go into the brains and strengthen them.

2. Vary this exercise by asking that the energy expand the consciousness and awareness levels in the brain.

Meditation 12: Developing
Spiritual Energy

1. Ask the energy of this sphere to turn to bliss, joy, or happiness, and fill the entire body.

2. Let the energy of this sphere go into the kundalini sphere and follow the instructions under step "e" in the kundalini meditations.

Heart Sphere

1. Battery source: Love

2. Purpose:

   - The ability to feel deep, pure love.

   - Brings understanding of others and your relationship to them.

   - Faith is strengthened and expanded.

   - Brings deep spiritual contentment.

   - Deep intuitions and awareness of coming changes, and what to do with them.

   - Brings out idealism, profoundness, great creativity, and action from the heart.

3. Negative side, when closed:

   - May be overwhelmed with love and unable to function.

   - Scrunching your shoulders can close off this sphere.

   - Heart and lung and other organ problems occur when closed.

   - The entire area may feel too open and vulnerable.

4. Meditations for Development:

Preparations for Meditation

    a. Focus of the heart sphere. Breathe into it.

    b. As you focus on this area, feel the energy of love, as the psychic-spiritual battery activating.

    c. Ask that the area be filled with prana.

    d. Bring the sexual energy into the area.

    e. Bring the earth energy into the area.

    f. Fill the area with an aqua color.

    g. Breathe in a rhythmic manner.

    h. Focus on the activating point.

Meditation 13: Love

Focus on the outlet point and ask to have the sphere filled with love.

1. Vary this exercise by thinking of friends, one at a time, and being open, in love, to let understanding of your relationship come to you.

2. Vary this exercise by asking the love vibration to expand to include faith.

3. Vary this exercise by asking the love to expand into spiritual commitment.

Meditation 14: Transcendence of the Heart

1. Focus on the outlet point and ask the intuitive energies to let you know of possible changes coming that you can be more aware of them.

2. Focus on the outlet point and ask the heart sphere to give you information on:

- Idealism

- Profoundness

- Creativity

- Actions you can take

Neck Sphere

1. Battery Source: Will

2. Purpose:

- Incredible strength to many levels, including physical, emotional, mental, and spiritual.

- Feeling "bigger than life," and very capable.

- By focusing on the wind, it can be stopped and started.

- Some people can keep machines running better by focusing on this area, and on the machine.

3. Negative Side, when closed:

- Your neck can feel clogged and rigid.

- Feeling bullnecked or stubborn.

4. Meditations for Development:

Preparations for Meditation

a. Focus on the neck sphere. Really let loose of neck muscles, so it can open well.

b. As you focus on this area, feel the energy of the will, as the psychic-spiritual battery, activating.

c. Ask the area to be filled with prana.

d. Bring sexual energy up from the sexual area.

e. Bring earth energy up through the feet into this area.

f. Fill the area with light blue.

g. Begin breathing gently in a rhythmic manner.

h. Focus on the outlet point for this sphere to help activate it.

Meditation 15: Strength and Variations

1. Focus on the outlet point and ask for strength to come in, fill this sphere, and then your entire body.

2. You may vary it by asking the energy to go to the physical, emotional, mental, or spiritual levels.

3. You may vary this exercise by asking rejuvenation energy to fill the physical body.

4. You may vary this exercise by asking the strength to go beyond the physical body and tap into energy around the body. This brings an expanded, "bigger-than-life" feeling.

Meditation 16: Working with Wind

Focus on the outlet point and ask the wind to stop or start. You may be asking, "Why do that?" It's part of our growth to work with forces of nature. Besides, it's wonderful to do when you are outdoors working on a hot, still day; a little breeze can be fabulous.

Meditation 17: Working with Machines

Focus on the outlet point and send strength to whatever machine you are working with. (Don't overdo until you find out how strong your energy is. You may blow out the machine.)

Mental Sphere

1. Battery Source: Mind

2. Purpose:

- Clear consciousness.

- Paranormal sight.

- Wit.

- Creative, inventive.

- Parallel dimensions.

- Comprehend this life as only a portion of your greater life.

- Clear visions.

3. Negative side, when closed:

- Headaches.

- Confusion.

- Health problems in the head.

- Trouble in seeing and hearing.

- Senses may feel "messed up."

- Head feels as though it's swimming inside.

- Inability to focus.

4. Meditations for Development:

Preparations for Meditation

a. Focus on the mental sphere, with the pineal gland being the center.

b. As you focus on this area, feel the energy of the mental psychic-spiritual battery activating.

c. Ask the area to be filled with prana.

d. Bring sexual energy from the sexual area to this sphere.

e. Bring earth energy up through the feet into this area.

f. Fill the area with a radiant light, with a very light yellow cast.

g. Begin breathing gently in a rhythmic manner.

h. Focus on the outlet point for this sphere to help activate it.

Meditation 18: Clear Consciousness with Variations

1. With your intent ask to see and feel the energy of clear consciousness.

2. With the clear consciousness, you may:

a. Ask to see into a parallel dimension to see something creative, or to be aware of an inventive idea and how to manifest them.

b. Ask for a clear vision of something to be achieved in the future.

c. Ask to see something humorous about life in general.

d. Ask to see or sense the greater reality of which we are all a part, and how our human life fits into it.

Higher Self Sphere

1. Battery Source: Soul

2. Purpose:

• Connection with the soul.

- Life is easier, and guidance is stronger and clearer.

- Transference of consciousness.

- Peace, it's above all.

- Higher perspective—cosmic view.

- Meditations that focus on this area greatly develop the soul.

- Recognizing the difference between destiny and karma, and recognizing others' karma and whether or not you need to be involved with it.

3. Negative side, when closed:

- Feelings of isolation, disconnectedness.

- No sense of purpose.

4. Meditations for Development:

Preparations for Meditation

a. Focus on the higher self sphere (located a distance equal to your height above your head. If, for example, you are five feet tall, then your higher self sphere would have its center about five feet above your head, if you were six feet tall it would be about six feet above you). If you ask your energy to focus in the higher self sphere and aim in that general direction, it will find the right place.

b. As you focus on this area, feel the energy of the psychic-spiritual battery, the soul and spirit energy, activating.

c. Ask the area to be filled with prana.

d. Bring sexual energy up from the sexual area.

e. Bring earth energy up through the feet into this area.

f. Fill the area with a radiant light.

g. Begin breathing gently in a rhythmic manner.

h. If you wish, focus on the outlet point for this sphere to help activate it.

Meditation 19: Connecting with the Soul Level

1. With your intent ask to feel a stronger connection with your soul.

2. Ask the soul's energies to come into your body and flood your system with its energy.

3. Ask for guidance or messages.

Meditation 20: Transference of Consciousness

Pho-wa, or transference of consciousness from the body to the higher self sphere or other areas, is something many people strive for. It is sometimes called an "out-of-the-body experience." It can be dangerous and should be undertaken with much care, as some people have died doing this. Their connection with the body becomes too thin and disappears. Another safer method is to focus partly on the higher self sphere, and to keep some consciousness still in the body. This is a dual awareness. The following is an exercise for this method:

1. With your intent, focus on the higher self sphere, ask a part of your consciousness to be in that sphere. Be open to experiences. When some of your consciousness is located there, you will be aware of other dimensions, have a heightened consciousness, and may achieve a cosmic consciousness.

2. With your intent, bring the expanded awareness into your body so that it can be experienced there, too. The ultimate is to have your system so clear and awake that you can experience these energies in your body, too.

Meditation 21: Enlightened Peace

1. With your intent focus on the higher self sphere.

2. Ask to feel the peace that comes from divine levels, and contains the qualities of enlightenment with it.

3. Bring this energy into your entire system and let it bathe all of your cells.

Meditation 22: Destiny and Karma

1. With your intent, focus on the higher self sphere.

2. Ask to feel the energy of destiny in your system. Ask what it is activating in your life at this time.

3. Ask to feel the energy of any karma active in your life at this time. Ask what it is, and how you can better deal with it.

The Silver Tube

There is an etheric silver tube about two inches in diameter running from the higher self sphere down through the body and into the earth. It sometimes is larger, and many times the area will be smaller. Sometimes it is damaged by misuse and incorrect flows. Sometimes it even curves. It should, however, be straight and even (see Figure 10.2, following page). The center of the tube is in front of the spine. This tube is used for the exchange of energies from one sphere to another. It is also used for energy to come down through the spheres, or up through the spheres, to

Figure 10.2 The Silver Tube

aid general development. The silver tube is also a connection for us with earth and spiritual energies. It is a very important part of our spherical system.

Although usually silver in color, it may sometimes be golden, or have other colors in it. Israel Regardie, in *The Middle Pillar,* calls this tube "the middle pillar," and refers to it as part of the tree of life. He gives much importance to it as a part of our general growth and development.

Meditation 23: Silver Tube

1. Visualize the silver tube from top to bottom. Does it appear to be in good shape, or does it need improving? Usually changing it with visualizations can accomplish the job. Sometimes healing energy needs to be sent. Meditating on the problems usually gives information.

2. Bring spiritual energy down through the tube, pausing to fill and activate each sphere, before moving on to the next one. When the meditation is completed, visualize the energy going into and through the earth, and back to the heavens.

Meditations Using All Spheres

The combined energy of all seven spheres can bring very powerful results in a number of areas. Practicing basic meditations using all seven can be a part of your regular practice, which will help in your overall development. It is important to have all spheres developed, since when one is shut down or underdeveloped, it has a tendency to slow down the others. Many times they work in unison, and that process would especially be hampered. The following are meditations using all seven of the spheres:

Meditation 24: Basic Seven Spheres

1. Focus on the seventh sphere. Imagine you are breathing into it as that will help bring prana into it and activate it.

2. Bring the energy from the seventh sphere through the silver tube into the sixth sphere, and so on, until the energy has reached the feet sphere.

3. Remain in a peaceful state, letting the energy of the spheres permeate your entire body.

Meditation 25: Centering and Strengthening

1. Be aware of the center of each sphere and the silver tube.

2. Imagine you are breathing into the center of each sphere, beginning with the feet and ending with all of them combined, with energy in the entire silver tube.

3. Bask in this combined energy until your awareness wavers, or you feel so energized you want to do something else. In either case, in the beginning, ten minutes would be sufficient as this can be quite powerful. For some, several minutes would be enough.

Meditation 26: Earth to Heaven and Back

1. Start with the feet sphere, and bring earth energy into it.

2. Bring the earth energy all the way up through the silver tube and into the other spheres up through the seventh sphere.

3. At the seventh sphere, release the earth energy and fill the sphere with spiritual energy.

4. Bring the spiritual energy into the silver tube, and then into each sphere, and on into the ground.

5. Remain in an open meditation for a few minutes.

Meditation 27: Samadhi and Bliss

Samadhi is a Sanskrit word that means "balance" or "evenness." When this state is reached, a person may experience various higher states or bliss.

1. Be aware of the center of each sphere.

2. Imagine you are breathing into the center of each sphere until they open up and feel activated. Feel energy in the silver tube.

3. Imagine you are floating, and that all spheres are equal.

4. Let your breathing be gentle.

5. Let your mind be still.

6. Experience the evenness.

7. Breathe out the sides of your chest, while maintaining the evenness.

8. Ask for the vibration of bliss to fill your spheres and your entire body.

Meditation 28: Qualities

The development of qualities is a very important part of our growth. This development affects the soul level and carries into other lives.

1. Focus on the center of the spheres.

2. Ask them to be filled with a quality. (This may include gentleness, love, strength, kindness, clarity, or whatever you prefer.)

3. Be in an open meditation and see what information comes to your consciousness.

Meditation 29: Drinking from the Well

1. Relax in a peaceful attitude.

2. Open all seven spheres and the silver tube. Imagine you are breathing deeply into all of them.

3. Have the feeling of drinking deeply from God's everlasting well, and let yourself be nourished by this energy. Let it flow through your entire body. Experience this for several minutes; a little longer if you can.

4. Be in an open meditation for five or ten minutes. See what information comes to you.

Meditation 30: Sharing Energy

1. Focus on the first sphere, located at the feet.

2. Open the energy and expand it all over your body.

3. Experience the quality of power of this energy in your body for a few minutes.

4. Focus on the other six spheres, in turn, then bringing the energy directly up the tube and also from sphere to sphere, following steps 2 and 3 with each.

5. Let all the spheres be open, with their energy flowing for a few minutes.

6. Be in an open meditation for five to ten minutes. Note whatever information comes to you.

The energies experienced in these mediations may be quite familiar to some of the readers, as the spheres can open spontaneously on their own. Taking time to make sure they are all functioning is well worth the time, as one's growth, development, and well-being are all enhanced by them.

Chapter 11

Using
the
Energies

ONCE THE LEVELS of consciousness have been opened, whether through the relentless push of evolution, or by your own diligent efforts to reach beyond the human energies, these energies will need to be used in daily life, as well as in meditation practices. They are usually developed through increased creativity, productivity, more altruistic philosophies, and greater mental and spiritual abilities. If one does not use these higher energies, they tend to back up in the system, sometimes causing illness or depression.

The best way to achieve your growth potential is to always push (appropriately) the edge of what you know and can achieve. Also take time to explore each thing you do to see if you can do it with more awareness and from a higher consciousness level, opening you to more choices.

Ask yourself how you can be more creative, how you can do your job or your projects in a more special way. Take time to meditate on your work or projects for a few minutes before you start—this can help you get into more efficient vibrations. Also, in your meditations, ask to see or know of better ways to do your planned task, and you may be surprised by the ideas that pour forth. Sometimes you have to be quiet and receptive for a while before information can be forthcoming. If you don't receive information in the first five minutes after asking, it may reveal itself to you at a later time.

Learning to do one's everyday tasks from a higher consciousness level is like developing your muscles; perhaps tiring at first, and perhaps leaving you not knowing what the results could be. If you don't develop and use your higher consciousness or spiritual energies in everyday living, then these energies aren't really assimilated and usable. What we do each day can be directed by our higher power.

If you have job, relationship, or personal difficulties, meditating on what greater possibilities are available in each situation can change the dynamics—just by being more aware. Greater knowledge usually makes major changes in your energy pattern right away, thus making change easier.

If you spend too much time trying to figure out the cause or past history of troublesome situations, it is possible to block new growth because your awareness is focused backwards into the past. Although this can be very helpful and should sometimes be looked at, too much looking back can be a block. Sometimes letting go of the past and turning one's energies into the future by looking at possible changes in patterns and new opportunities can be more beneficial.

Overall Development

Meditation is a form of higher mental and spiritual exercise. These areas need exercise and stimulation as much as the physical, emotional, and mental areas do. Some people like to take meditations from books such as this one and incorporate them into their daily routines. Others like to work with a particular set of exercises until some mastery is gained over them, and then shift to other things. Whatever process or material you choose, it should give enough variety so you don't become stuck on your path. If so, the path becomes a rut and development becomes lopsided, and this takes balance out of your life.

Greeting each experience with awareness and sensitivity will help new learning unfold. It's fine to do a number of things, such as brushing your teeth, from an habitual space. However, if too much of life is lived in an unaware habitual pattern, more and more awareness and understanding are blocked. Life itself becomes blocked and eventually, from lack of growth experience, existence can become pretty grim and negative. In this case, opening up to life could be quite painful.

This book is designed somewhat as a reference manual and can be used privately or in groups. The meditations are listed for easy reference. It can be helpful as a part of overall growth to have a number of such books for different areas. Varying exercises can help keep you from getting stuck on your path, especially if you are working alone in your growth, a variety of exercises to choose from can help keep freshness in your practice.

Lightness of Energy

There is a problem with this New Spirituality, however. For maximum benefit, you will need to have lighter vibrations and not let yourself be weighed down with worry and other heavy energies. If your energies are heavy or you try to live your life as usual, it will be more difficult to solve problems, since solutions will come from the lighter, finer energies. Life will seem more chaotic and unmanageable. Developing your spiritual abilities will help you handle these exciting new energies. Take time to let new philosophies and new ideas come into you. Pay more attention to your experiences and intuitions. Take time each day to be lighter, and this will allow the new energies to come in more freely.

As part of your growth you may wish to spend some time working specifically on systems that deal with the vibrations of sevens and twelves as a way of activating the benefits of their numerological energies within you. Just being open to these higher energies can bring greater development. This would need to be balanced with other exercises, however, so as not to get too structured in one area. If any pattern becomes too burdensome or boring, then it is time to make a change, as you may have overdeveloped in one area. Some like to take one area and focus completely on that. It does sometimes catapult a person into higher levels. However, with our energies as they are now (very Aquarian; that is, expansive and revolutionary) it is usually best to have a variety. No matter how you plan your growth, remembering to enjoy your path is a great way to keep your resolve.

Appendix

Spherical Cleansing Chart

This chart may be used by someone leading a cleansing, or doing a cleansing for yourself.

Cleansing For: _____

Sphere Quadrant: _____

1. Color(s): _____

2. Thoughts, Feelings, or Pictures: _____

_____

_____

_____

3. This life _____ or past life _____

4. Seed Incident:_____

_____

_____

_____

5. Learning or Purpose:

_____

_____

_____

a. If the situation is a difficult or negative one, fill the area with a lavender color and blessings. Then ask the lavender for a message:

_____

b. If the situation is a positive one, fill the area with radiance and blessings. Then ask the radiance for a message:

_____

6. Fill the quadrant with thanks.

Glossary

Auras: Subtle energy emanations from various bodies. The energy manifests in colors, sensations, and sometimes patterns. They appear around the physical body.

Akashic Records: Akasha is an energy upon which records are imprinted of our lives, past, present, and probable futures, are imprinted.

Brains:

Reptilian—This brain has to do with our basic instincts of survival and territory. It relates to the physical body.

Limbic System—This brain system relates to our emotions and motivations, and to the emotional body.

Neo-mammalian—This system consists of the left and right brains and the corpus callosum. It relates to the mental body.

Etheric Brains—These brains have not manifested into physical matter. These brains are a connecting link to higher manifestations of mental and spiritual energy and allow us to function in higher dimensions. These brains relate to bodies four through seven. It is possible that a physical connection will manifest some day.

Bliss: A higher state of consciousness in which a person experiences joyful or ecstatic feelings.

Bodies: Bodies are masses of energy vibrating at particular speeds. Each body, through its vibrational level, becomes a vehicle through which a particular state of consciousness can express. Each body operates at a higher vibration than the one previous to it.

Physical—This is the densest body and most relates to action. It is the only body easily seen.

Emotional/Astral—Feelings are from this level. Motivation also comes from this body.

Mental—Thoughts are processed in this body as well as other mental activities occur here.

Intuitional/Compassionate—Compassion and intuition emanate from the vibrations of this body.

Will/Spirit—Personal spirit and will are expressed through the vibrations of this body.

Soul Level—The energies of this body resonate with our eternal soul. Our "I Am-ness" is expressed through this body.

Divine Level—The energies of this body resonate with divine levels. Our connection with our Creator is most easily felt here.

Higher Self: A part of ourselves which is the connecting link between personalities and souls.

Inner World: This is the area deep in our psyche that relates to mysticism, shamanism, mythology, the subconscious, and collective unconsciousness. It is as intricate and expansive as is our outer world.

Karma: This is an energy which forces actions, thoughts, and feelings to balance. It is a strong tool for growth as it continually pushes us towards a spiritual life through balancing positive and negative forces.

Kundalini: This is an evolutionary energy which enters the physical body through the kundalini gland located between the anus and the genitals. When awakened, it can be forceful and painful as it goes through a person's system, cleansing and refining the cells and lifting a person to higher consciousness.

Nadis: These are nerve-like filaments located in the etheric body through which prana, kundalini, and other subtle energies flow.

Pho-Wa: The art of out-of-body travel.

Planes: These are vibratory levels of energy in our cosmos. Our bodies relate to these planes, such as, the physical body relates to the physical plane. The emotional or astral body relates to the astral plane. The mental relates to the mental plane, etc.

Prana: This is a life force which has a number of levels of manifestation. Life is dependent upon it. It emanates from the sun.

Samadhi: This is a state of evenness or balance from which things may manifest. In its higher level it is the state of bliss.

Silver Tube: This is a tube made of psycho-spiritual energy through which energies travel to connect the spherical system. It usually is silver in color, although, it may at times have golden or other hues.

Spheres: These are part of the spherical system and contain energies which can help in bringing health, peace, and well-being to a person. When more fully developed, they have energies which are quite magical and can manifest such things as tumo, clear vision, transcendence, and other gifts.

Thought Forms: These are energy patterns which contain a person's strong thoughts. These thought forms can hang around a person, be left hanging wherever a person put them out of his or her mind, or sent to others. They are usually grayish or may be a dark indigo cast, unless very well defined in which case they may be colors and geometric shapes. Usually, they are similar to cloud formations and may be a foot or two in diameter.

Value Sensors: These are the part of our senses which interprets information they have received and let us know if there is value or not. Value sensors also warn of danger or fearful things.

Vitality Globules: These contain prana from the sun before it is broken down into its various levels. They are minute in size and can sometimes be seen dancing in the sunlight by the naked eye. Some people are able to see them. We take them in through our breath, our skin, and our chakras. Some are in food and water as well. Fresh food still has lots of prana in it. Our spleen breaks the prana into their various levels and distributes them throughout our bodies.

Web: The web is made of etheric material and is around our bodies. It protects us from excessively strong energies.

Bibliography

Cavendish, Richard, ed. *Man, Myth and Magic,* Vol. 18. Marshall Cavendish Corporation: New York, NY. 1970.

——. *Man, Myth and Magic,* Vol. 21. Marshall Cavendish Corporation: New York, NY. 1970.

Evans-Wentz, W. Y., ed. *Tibetan Yoga and Secret Doctrines.* Oxford University Press: London, Oxford, New York. 1971.

Javane, Faith and Dusty Bunker. *Numerology and the Divine Triangle.* Whitford Press: West Chester, PA. 1979.

Leadbeater, C. W. *Man Visible and Invisible.* The Theosophical Publishing House: Wheaton, IL. 1969.

Paulson, Genevieve Lewis. *Energy-Focused Meditation* (formerly titled *Meditation and Human Growth*). Llewellyn Publications: St. Paul, MN. 1997 and 2000.

———. *Kundalini and the Chakras*. Llewellyn Publications: St. Paul, MN. 1992.

Paulson, Genevieve Lewis and Stephen J. Paulson. *Reincarnation: Remembering Past Lives*. Llewellyn Publications: St. Paul, MN. 1997.

Regardie, Israel. (Chic Cicero and Sandra Tabatha Cicero, eds.) *The Middle Pillar*. Llewellyn Publications: St. Paul, MN. 1998.

Index

☽ REACH FOR THE MOON

Llewellyn publishes hundreds of books on your favorite subjects! To get these exciting books, including the ones on the following pages, check your local bookstore or order them directly from Llewellyn.

ORDER BY PHONE

- Call toll-free within the U.S. and Canada, 1-800-THE MOON
- In Minnesota, call (651) 291-1970
- We accept VISA, MasterCard, and American Express

ORDER BY MAIL

- Send the full price of your order (MN residents add 7% sales tax) in U.S. funds, plus postage & handling to:

    Llewellyn Worldwide
    P.O. Box 64383, Dept. 1-56718-513-4
    St. Paul, MN 55164–0383, U.S.A.

POSTAGE & HANDLING

(For the U.S., Canada, and Mexico)

- $4.00 for orders $15.00 and under
- $5.00 for orders over $15.00
- No charge for orders over $100.00

We ship UPS in the continental United States. We ship standard mail to P.O. boxes. Orders shipped to Alaska, Hawaii, The Virgin Islands, and Puerto Rico are sent first-class mail. Orders shipped to Canada and Mexico are sent surface mail.

International orders: Airmail—add freight equal to price of each book to the total price of order, plus $5.00 for each non-book item (audio tapes, etc.).

Surface mail—Add $1.00 per item.

Allow 2 weeks for delivery on all orders.
Postage and handling rates subject to change.

DISCOUNTS

We offer a 20% discount to group leaders or agents. You must order a minimum of 5 copies of the same book to get our special quantity price.

Visit our web site at www.llewellyn.com for more information.

Kundalini and the Chakras

A Practical Manual—
Evolution in this Lifetime

Genevieve Lewis Paulson

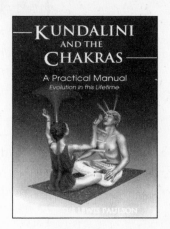

The mysteries of Kundalini revealed! We all possess the powerful evolutionary force of Kundalini that can open us to genius states, psychic powers, and cosmic consciousness. As the energies of the Aquarian Age intensify, more and more people are experiencing the "big release" spontaneously but have been ill-equipped to channel its force in a productive manner. This book shows you how to release Kundalini gradually and safely, and is your guide to sating the strange, new appetites which result when life-in-process "blows open" your body's many energy centers.

The section on chakras brings new understanding to these "dials" on our life machine (body). It is the most comprehensive information available for cleansing and developing the chakras and their energies. Read *Kundalini and the Chakras* and prepare to make a quantum leap in your spiritual growth!

0-87542-592-5, 224 pp., 6 x 9, illus., color plates $14.95

Energy Focused Meditation
Body, Mind, Spirit

Genevieve Lewis Paulson

Meditation has many purposes: healing, past life awareness, balance, mental clarity, and relaxation. It is a way of opening into areas that are beyond your normal thinking patterns. In fact, what we now call "altered states" and "peak experiences"—tremendous experiences of transcendental states—can become normal occurrences when you know how to contact the higher energy vibrations.

Most people think that peak experiences happen, at best, only a few times in life. Through meditation, however, it is possible to develop your higher awareness so you can bring more peak happenings about by concentrated effort. *Energy Focused Meditation* is full of techniques for those who wish to claim those higher vibrations and expanded awareness for their lives today.

1-56718-512-6, 224 pp., 6 x 9, 17 illus.   **$12.95**

Reincarnation

Remembering Past Lives

Genevieve Lewis Paulson
& Stephen J. Paulson

Why is knowledge of your past lives of any value to your present life? Traumatic events from the past can create blocks to your current growth and joys. Attitudes can carry over that hold you back from healthy relationships. Irrational fears with no known cause can sometimes be traced back to events in previous lives.

Reincarnation shows you how to enter into your own meditative state and access your own experiences and knowledge. Explore your cycles of lives . . . soul mates and soul relationships . . . soul families and tribes . . . the akashic records . . . genetic influences . . . the many facets of karma and how to transmute it . . . the process of evolution . . . leading past life regressions for others . . . how to die gracefully . . . finding your soul teacher . . . opening to your intuition . . . and much more.

1-56718-511-8, 224 pp., 5 ³/₁₆ x 8, illus.   **$7.95**

To order call 1-800-THE MOON
(Prices subject to change without notice)

The Energy Body Connection

The Healing Experience of Self-Embodiment

Pamela Welch, M.A.

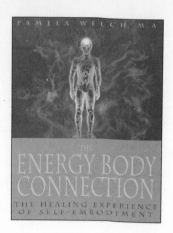

Illness, unresolved emotional issues, and mental patterns that no longer serve you are actually coded messages from your own soul. *The Energy Body Connection* teaches you the truth about these major soul imprints and shows you how to break the code!

This embodiment process acknowledges emotions and physical problems as signposts of transformation. Instead of denying them, you can restructure their energy patterns, awakening your body's cells and tissues through the infusion of a spiritual presence.

Powerful exercises in each chapter help you to discover the meaning of your essential soul patterns, experience your chakra energy centers, direct your consciousness to obtain the results you desire, listen to your body's wisdom, access the healing messages contained in your dreams, work with healing light and color, and meet your spirit guides.

1-56718-819-2, 360 pp., 6 x 9 $14.95